I0834691

ENDORSEMENTS

I have been in ministry almost 30 years, and I have never met anyone with greater love and passion for the Lord than my wife, Amy. Equally as important in her life is her reverence for God's word, both written and spoken. I have witnessed the Lord conveying to her profound spiritual truths as well as insights and counsel throughout day-to-day activities. Her life is a true example of what it means to live in the realm of the Spirit and walk with God. It has been very rewarding for me to watch her deposit in print, through her captivating writing style, the divine encounters that she has had in the realm of God's knowledge and also the spirit of might. I was present when she experienced an amazing visitation, being taken into the realm of the spirit of knowledge. I heard the reverence in her voice as she shared those revelations and the deep truth that came from it. I was there when she experienced the spirit of might and the revelation of God's rest that comes from abiding with Him. I heard her share firsthand what it means to be tethered to the Lord and the promise of God to remove from His people the veil of ignorance. All of these incredible insights are shared within the pages of this book through the vocabulary of the Spirit. It is a call to the remnant of God's people to experience end-of-the-age enlightenment, latter-rain revelation poured out to a company of people desperate to encounter the Lord in this dimension of His Spirit. *Divinely Powerful* is a great tool to help people access God's unseen realm and experience what has been allotted as meat in due season. I am completely confident that the readers of this book will be taken on a prophetic journey into God's presence and will draw from the treasures found in the reverential awe of the Lord. These will provide keys that give us access to God's heart and His profound provision for this hour.

PAUL KEITH DAVIS
WhiteDove Ministries

Amy Thomas Davis has captured God's heart for this new era in her book *Divinely Powerful.* Amy opens a spiritual window to catch glimpses of the unseen realm and thinning veil between Heaven and earth. She has developed a pathway for us to learn language that communicates the very essence of Heaven's reflection, experiencing His power and authority in this final harvest on this earth. *Divinely Powerful* serves as a guide to give us insight as we journey forward, giving us blueprints and windows to see into the Spirit realm, discovering things to come and mysteries God is revealing in this hour. Amy's insight and instruction teaches us how to position ourselves as true messengers of hope and connect our hearts with the reverential fear of the Lord. I highly recommend *Divinely Powerful* as a must-read as we prepare our hearts and minds and adjust our lives to the rhythm of Heaven.

CINDY MCGILL
Hope for the Harvest Ministries

Amy Thomas Davis has done a great job encapsulating the blueprint for the next move of God. She articulates so well from the Spirit of revelation on subjects rarely discussed in the Body of Christ. The material in this book is so incredibly presented that it had to be divinely inspired. I strongly recommend all to read this book and reread it until you fully absorb its content.

Chris Reed
MorningStar Ministries

Divinely Powerful by Amy Thomas Davis is one of the most important books of our time. It contains essential perspective from the heart of God for this hour that not only informs but activates. I encourage you to open your heart as you journey through these powerful pages, allowing the author's words to bring forth divine alignment within you. Fresh hope and strength will begin to rise, enabling you to take your position in the greatest time in human history.

Everything is about to change! The manifest glory of God we have hoped for is about to consume the earth. The great unveiling of Christ within His people is upon us.

As the ancient prophets foretold, the Shining Ones are now on earth. All that Jesus held in His heart for you and for this planet before the world was formed is about to be made manifest. This is your moment to step in.

Liz Wright
International Bestselling Author of *Reflecting God*

Amy Thomas Davis is one of the purest prophets of this generation and much loved around the world. She speaks with sweetness, compassion, and hope that touches the heart. I believe she is part of a new generation of oracle voices God is releasing to the earth to help us get ready for the next age. I am so glad Amy has written down her profound revelations and insights with God in this unique book at this specific moment in history. I saw angels being released over people as they read this book. We are ready for more!

JUSTIN PAUL ABRAHAM
Company of Burning Hearts

DIVINELY POWERFUL

A PROPHETIC BLUEPRINT INTRODUCING THE COMING AGE

AMY THOMAS DAVIS

DESTINY IMAGE® PUBLISHERS, INC.
P.O. Box 310, Shippensburg, PA 17257-0310
"Promoting Inspired Lives."

This book and all other Destiny Image and Destiny Image Fiction books are available at Christian bookstores and distributors worldwide.

Cover design by Eileen Rockwell
Interior design by Terry Clifton

For more information on foreign distributors, call 717-532-3040.
Reach us on the Internet: www.destinyimage.com.

ISBN 13 TP: 978-0-7684-6100-8
ISBN 13 eBook: 978-0-7684-6101-5
ISBN 13 HC: 978-0-7684-6103-9
ISBN 13 LP: 978-0-7684-6102-2

For Worldwide Distribution.
1 2 3 4 5 6 7 8 / 25 24 23 22 21

Dedicated to my loving husband, who encouraged me to dream and write and dream again: I do not fly without you.

To my amazing kids, Elissa and Elijah. Always remember who you are. You are loved. You are free.

To all of my friends and family who stood with me in the darkest night: I'll never forget your love.

And of course, to all the overcomers: This book is dedicated to you. You will tell the story of the brightest day.

CONTENTS

FOREWORD

We have entered into a new era, and we are moving into uncharted territory as the Body of Christ. We are going where we have never gone before, the days ahead with Christ, are truly exciting. The glorious displays of His majesty, His power, and His presence that will be seen will be like nothing we have ever seen before. In this new era, the Lord is calling us deeper into the depths of His heart and deep place of intimacy. There is a heralding invitation to "know His ways" and to partner with Him in the new thing that He is doing (Isa. 43:19).

I remember so clearly the whisper of the Holy Spirit to me when He began to unpack His heart to me about this new era: "You have not been this way before." The sense surrounded me so strongly that in a new era, there are new blueprints, new strategies, new wineskins, and new pathways in partnering with the Lord.

> *Make me to know Your ways, O Lord; teach me Your paths* (Psalm 25:4).

The Lord is looking for those who will sit at His feet, like Mary, and absorb every revelation that He is releasing (see Luke 10). The ones who will seek the Lord for His wisdom and understanding for this new era. To be so deeply connected in oneness and union with Him, hearing the symphony of His heart and stepping into the divine dance with Him in the new ways He is leading, this is the place He is calling us into. The deeper place of yielded surrender. The deeper place of consecration and radical abandonment unto Him. Overwhelmed, overcome, filled and burning with the revelation of our beautiful Jesus and His fiery, passionate, all-consuming love for His people. It is time for His people to arise from a place of deep, yielded surrender to Him, to a greater place of living by the Spirit and not from the soul (see Isa. 60:1). It is a place of communion, deeper than we have ever known.

A remnant is arising in the earth who live in the awe and wonder of who He is—living in the reverential fear of the Lord, walking in holiness and purity as they daily encounter His goodness and locked with His fiery eyes of love as they move into the era of the greatest move of God that has ever been seen.

The realm of revelation that is upon us will allow us to access the blueprints of the Lord as He reveals His deep mysteries. In this stunning new era, we will not only recognize the time and the season in which we live like the sons of Issachar but receive the wisdom and understanding to partner with the revelation the Lord is releasing.

This incredible book by my friend Amy Thomas Davis is such an incredible gift to you and to the Body of Christ. The encounters that Amy shares in this incredible book carry a deep impartation for you for this new era. *Divinely Powerful* is not only a treasure chest of deep wisdom for you to glean on and partner with what the Lord is going to do—it is a gift to you to help you navigate the "ways" of the Lord and His heart. Even as I printed the pages of this glorious manuscript to read for this foreword, I could feel the anointing upon each page. This book drips with the oil of intimacy, been birthed by having someone who lives close to the heart of Jesus and is a friend of God.

I believe that you will encounter such powerful waves of His Spirit as you read these pages. *Divinely Powerful* will bring greater awakening, healing, deliverance, and understanding to you, to empower you to walk in greater revelation and understanding of what the Lord is preparing us, His Bride, for in this new era.

As His people, we are going to be reintroduced to His power as He displays His majesty in ways we have never seen before. As the Holy Spirit invites you into deeper depths of revelation and understanding in these pages, you will see the beautiful divine road map the Lord has placed in your hands through this incredible book, to move with Jesus into the uncharted territories He has for you.

I believe as I was, the love of God will grip your heart deeply as you read through these pages. This is not a book to read once, this is a "continue to refer back to" book for the new era. Amy has articulated the Lord's heart and His truth with such purity, accuracy, and authority such that, by His Spirit, you will be branded and marked afresh with revival fire and hunger to follow Jesus and walk in all He has for you.

There are divine appointments for you with the Lord contained within these pages. This book is as a trumpet, announcing the era of God's people walking in greater power and authority from the place of deep communion with Him. Will you answer the call?

The greatest days of His majesty displayed, power revealed, and Kingdom extended are upon us. Will you take your place? He is calling you deeper.

Lana Vawser
Lana Vawser Ministries
Author of *The Prophetic Voice of God, A Time to Selah*, and *I Hear the Lord Say, New Era*

INTRODUCTION

In the coming days, a people will shine like the brightness of the expanse of Heaven and lead the many to righteousness like the stars forever and ever (see Dan. 12:3).

I am excited for the opportunity to share the story of this bright day. It has taken a few dark days to get here, but the hour has come. The hour that the heroes of the faith have prophesied about is here. The hour when a generation is enlightened and tastes the good Word of God and the powers of the age to come (see Heb. 6). In a vibrant display of His glory, we will bring in the greatest harvest the world has ever seen.

The pages of this book are printed in fire and blood, which is truth and love. They are printed with the future of the remnant in mind and the light miracles they will execute. God is the Creator of these blueprints; I was simply the pen of a ready writer.

I love to know the story behind a story. Let me share with you what was happening while I was journaling these prophetic insights.

I was in Alabama with a purpose to write. While we were there, I got sick and was put in quarantine. I was fighting the coronavirus and had a very bad bacterial infection. This was my second bout with this virus, and it hit me differently than the first time. I was in excruciating pain and did not eat for over a week. I had just healed from shingles weeks earlier.

I remained in quarantine for the duration of our time in Alabama. While I was hidden away, we were hit by a hurricane. This was the second hurricane to hit the condo in Alabama since I started this project.

There was warfare back in Oregon too. The warfare, the hurricane, and the virus did not stop me, and they did not stop the Lord. I had waited long and traveled far to hear from God. I knew the Lord had revelation for His remnant. I had seen in my visions that He was going to meet with me in this place. And meet with me He did.

As I proceeded to write, a portal of revelation opened in the Spirit realm in the dining room of that Alabama condo. That is where I wrote my favorite chapters of this book. Of course, I love every revelation, and each chapter has a story behind the story—some were written long before they were compiled here. They are drenched in prayers and tears. But you will know my favorite chapters, for you will feel the fire on the pages.

CHAPTER 1

THE SPIRIT OF KNOWLEDGE

It was summertime in Orange Beach, Alabama. I encountered a realm purely of the Spirit. I was taken there several times. The atmosphere was intense and immovable. I am still unraveling its mysteries. This realm carries an infinite message. I was given a portion to prophesy to His Beloved. I have had many revelatory encounters with the Lord; the prophecy I will share is a culmination of them all. I am honored to share these encounters. It is the greatest story I have ever known. I hope to express its essence in words not taught by human wisdom but in those taught by the Spirit, combining spiritual thoughts with spiritual words (see 1 Cor. 2).

Here it is, one message, and it must be displayed in great reverence:

THE TRUE KNOWLEDGE OF GOD

That summer evening, the Spirit of the Lord brought me into the realm of His knowledge. I entered into the unseen realm three times and returned to our bed three times. Each time I returned, I had learned a little more. Eventually, I understood the Kingdom I was in and how I got there. It was my great privilege to stand on the fringes of the spirit of knowledge.

The journey leading up to this encounter had been tumultuous. I was drawn into the spirit of knowledge through hardship, pain, and perseverance.

I had been contending to rise above the torment of the second heavens. Longing to escape the seemingly endless battle, I traveled back and forth between worry's burden and the breath of life. I felt trapped in the depths as though imprisoned in the bottom of a sea. I would press my way to the surface of the deep where my lips would touch the rim for a moment. Opening my lungs, I would draw a breath before being pulled back under again. Temporary relief was not sufficient; the grace for this season had faded. I knew the ways of a warrior. Moving in traditional spiritual warfare, I had worked incessantly to destroy every lofty thing raised up against the truth, but this battle had changed me and weakened my authority.

Unaware of the massive transformation that was about to take place in and through me, I moved forward courageously. In my prayer space, I reached for Him in deep longing for communion—to eat of His flesh and drink of His blood. I petitioned the Lord for a revelation that would make this simple soul operate in dimensions of wisdom and authority that surpass human understanding.

I had been in the resurrection process, but I was waiting for my identity in Him. I was coming alive again. I know now that the realm of the spirit of knowledge continues to show me who He is and, therefore, who I am. Identity is a motivator of resurrection power. It is a mystery revealed in the spirit of knowledge.

Later that evening, after many hours of meditation, a presence entered. An atmosphere resembling a star-filled sky covered the room from wall to wall. The Creator of the universe came and stayed awhile, beckoning me into light. It felt as though I was corralled with His glory. True knowledge began to fill the space around me. He was guiding me into a new dimension. I had tasted the direction and eaten His Word. What did this light have for me now?

I had left the toxic atmosphere. The dimension of light awaited my visitation. I could feel its pull on my chest like a piercing, even *"as far as the division of soul and spirit, of both joints and marrow"* (Heb. 4:12). The impression of abounding thunder shook me to my core. I had left "time" and entered the glory of another realm, the realm of the spirit of knowledge.

It felt as though the Lord had ceased time to bring me into a hidden place encountered only by the sons of God. I was drawn into a dimension where peace is complete. This is the Kingdom where glory dwells. I struggle to express the magnitude of His design. Who could describe deity unmatchable? I understand why unwritten revelations are recorded in the private place and concealed until the fullness of time. Perhaps it is far too much for a soul to bear.

THE DOOR

The door between this land and the heart of my Father is very thin, though accessing it is not an easy venture. I entered through a gateway to get to the realm of the spirit of knowledge. This gateway is made up of two layers with a room in between. These layers were something like skin or a soft skin-like chrysalis. I have heard people describe this door as a veil. That is the only language I had for it. But these layers of skin did not resemble a typical veil as we would understand it.

I entered rather quickly through the first layer; it felt as though I was pushed through a birth canal into a new dimension. Even so, this was the easiest layer. I knew in my spirit that this dimension is the realm of "the change." This "change" is not like deliverance but rather transformation into glory. Paul describes it in 2 Corinthians 3:17-18:

> *Now the Lord is the Spirit, and where the Spirit of the Lord is, there is liberty. But we all, with unveiled face, beholding as in a mirror the glory of the Lord, are being transformed into the same*

> *image from glory to glory, just as from the Lord, the Spirit.*

I entered through the first layer complete with thoughts and emotions. Once I had entered, I remained in what seemed like a vestibule or an antechamber of the Lord's palace; this is where I went through a cleaning process, but only for a moment, for another layer quickly engaged me. The cleaning process was in between two layers. It was quick and fairly painless. At this point, I had no conscious thought of where I was or where I was going. It seemed to be a place seldom journeyed.

Finally, I made it to the next portion of the doorway. However, the second layer was an agonizing process, separating my soul from spirit.

To go beyond into the palace of His heart, I would have to leave a few things behind. I left my conscious thoughts, will, and emotions. My soul's unsanctified opinion is not relevant in the land of Love's heart. This final layer of chrysalis painfully and graciously separated my soul and left it at the foot of the door.

I came to understand that the entrance to the spirit of knowledge is a door of hope—the perfect design to prepare me to dwell in the secret place. The gateway is His Word.

> *For the word of God is living and active and sharper than any two-edged sword, and piercing as far as the division of soul and spirit,*

> *of both joints and marrow, and able to judge the thoughts and intentions of the heart. And there is no creature hidden from His sight, but all things are open and laid bare to the eyes of Him with whom we have to do* (Hebrews 4:12-13).

Being stretched and separated by the power of His Word is both exquisite and terrifying. It is both perfect peace and the fear of the Lord simultaneously. I find myself encompassed by the dangers of this love, marveling at such perfect design. His Spirit must permeate my soul, or my soul could never bear His glory.

The Veil Is Thin

I had a growing desire to stay in this unseen realm forever. I went back and forth three times. Each time I returned, I hollered tearfully, "The veil is thin! The veil is thin!" Reverential awe consumed me, increasing with each visitation. I longed to step in deeper, though I never went beyond the fringes.

I was drawn through the same process at the gate each time I went in. The process did become easier. Still, the separation of soul from spirit was never absent of pain.

I had a growing understanding of the kindness and severity of God. Being encountered by the One who clears the heavens by His breath and quiets the sea with His power (see Job 26) increased the reverential fear in my soul. I know without a doubt that I am an awe-inspired lover of the highest God. I explained this revelation in this journal entry I wrote the morning following the experience:

> I am an ensouled being, but now I understand the necessity of the Spirit more fully, filling this soul to the fullness, into every member. There are realms of His Spirit which human language cannot define, nor soul alone can stand before. There are realms only interpreted in awe and expressed through reverent submission to the Most High.
>
> The unwritten revelation can be accessed, but for now, it remains a message without words. As His Spirit fills us to the fullness, we will begin to go and access the seven realms even beyond the fringes. Seven spirits are connected to the seven thunders. The seven thunders are an infilling that the soul cannot interpret and opinions cannot create.

I was truly brushing against the heart of the Lord, a chamber room vast and immovable. I had been granted access to a glorious realm beyond human grasp. While I was experiencing transformation and receiving revelation, my husband, Paul Keith, was contending on my behalf.

He took his stand against massive anaconda-like serpents in filthy knee-deep swamp water. These demonic creatures swarmed him, attacking from all sides. He would fight one off, then quickly turn to fight the next. Battling against three different serpents, he continued to hold them off, perhaps so that I could enter the unseen realm of God three different times.

There was a very tangible battle happening in our midst. The winds and the deeps roared through our room while the thunders shook the atmosphere above us. His battle stance in the trenches is a beautiful description of a true forerunner, trudging through the mire and the muck so that those following can journey into glory.

We are forever grateful for the revelation that inspired awe and changed everything. This verse in the book of Job describes what Paul Keith and I encountered and what was happening in the spirit realm. From the fleeing serpent to the sound of thunders and the fringes of His ways:

> *By His breath the heavens are cleared; His hand has pierced the fleeing serpent. Behold, these are the fringes of His ways; and how faint a word we hear of Him! But His mighty thunder, who can understand?* (Job 26:13-14)

THE YIELDING CHAMBER

There is a vast glory and eternal revelation that will form our opinion from the wisdom of another realm. This opinion is absent of fear and fully motivated by love.

I had gone back and forth into the unseen through His Word. I learned quickly that the least painful way to access this realm is by yielding up my spirit. My will and opinions were the most difficult to release, but they are not permitted or necessary in this place. Yielding was the only access through the gate and was a reality of this dimension.

I wanted desperately to bring this dimension back to earth. I tried to pull on it as though it were movable. This was the most painful part of all. I thought my heart would be torn out. The physical pain lingered for days. That dimension gripped and stretched me thin. I believe it was part of the process of learning to yield as He removed that which can be shaken, as of created things, so that those which cannot be shaken may remain.

Submission is an acceptable service to God offered up in gratitude with reverence and awe, for our God is a consuming fire.

In releasing my own story, I received the revelation of the greatest story, that which is authored by God and continuing to be revealed (see Heb. 12).

The submission is not something I can explain sufficiently, though it is easily understood through the spirit of revelation. I do not even know that I have a conscious memory of it, though my spirit knows it well. It was the piercing of a double-edged sword dividing sinew from the bone. It was being laid bare, entering rest, and being known.

During this encounter, I learned quickly to separate my opinion from His reality. This is a heavenly concept that exposes new dimensions of this unseen realm. We do not experience the fullness of the knowledge of God through our might, opinions, or expectations. We experience it by yielding up our spirit.

THE SEVENFOLD SPIRIT OF GOD

There are seven spirits of God: the spirit of the Lord, the spirit of wisdom and understanding, the spirit of counsel and might, the spirit of knowledge, and the reverential fear of the Lord (see Isa. 11:2). The seven spirits of God are the realms of perfect love, each dimension incomprehensible by the human mind. It is full, lovely, mysteriously compelling, and remarkable—eternal, with no beginning and no end. Paul Keith describes the seven spirits of God like this:

> God's "Sevenfold Spirit" is a wonderful mystery to highlight the functioning of the Lord's Spirit in the earth. It is not in contradiction to the triune nature of God but a perfect and complete expression of His Spirit that demonstrates the fullness of His character and power. The Spirit of the Lord does not have wisdom and revelation, counsel and might, knowledge and reverential awe; He is all of these.

This humbling encounter with the Spirit of the Lord revealed insight and strategy only found in the heart of God. Having been drawn in through the Word gave me the realization that I could enter into the Word at any moment. That means we do not simply read the Word. We actually have the ability to go in it!

Even from the realm of time, I can go into His Word. Beyond the simple execution of declaring the Word and praying, this approach will bring transformation.

It is different from a conversation with the Lord during a time of prayer. I appreciate these precious moments and have found extreme value in sharing my heart with my Beloved.

We have become accustomed to asking questions and waiting for answers regarding temporal situations. In fear, we plead with God to fix what seems essential at the time. When the Lord draws near, we push aside our questions and tuck away with Him. Sometimes we emotionally lay out all our questions. I have seen many people try mindfully to visit the Lord in their imagination. The eternal realm is not like the prayer room described above; the temporal is not a burden there. I did not have a conscious reality to push away thoughts, opinions, worries, and imaginations; I simply was not able to have them. I journaled it like this:

> The presence of God both inspires and is inspired by awe. We are growing in incredible

> desperation to go beyond the veil and engage the seven spirits of God. If we only use our "imaginations" to access these heavenly places, we are usually tapping into our soul instead of drawing heavenly perspective from realms unseen and accessed only through the living Word. In the place of supercilious imaginations, there is little reverence for the Lord Jesus Christ, who paid a perfect price so we can access the Father through His blood and the reverential fear of the Lord. The greatest transformation is not accessed in vain imaginations; but by reverence, we will call in the very wind of Heaven. Divine revelation and a true encounter with God will always bring great change and activate life within us. We will be blessed with greater authority and responsibility.

THE THUNDER

During this experience, my husband and I both heard the roar of His thunder like the sound of His Word when it penetrates your soul. The thunders were both a sight and a sound, revealing that a mystery was available to ponder. The sound of thunder quickly drew me in; I recognized that a place exists in another realm, and it is open to my visitation. This place is far beyond a simple reverie; it is the place of true knowledge where awestruck lovers learn their way.

> *When the sound of the trumpet grew louder and louder, Moses spoke and God answered him with thunder* (Exodus 19:19).

One year later, I had a separate encounter that brought understanding that a resurrected prayer life is available to us through communion with the Lord. The voice of thunder had returned. I had complete knowledge of it dropping through the ceiling in our room. I felt it pressing toward me as though it would go in me and never stop to hover. I quickly dove into the thunder without restraint. Navigation was unnecessary; this time, my spirit knew how to enter.

I went into the washing place. The washing place is beautiful. In a moment, the world's hurts are washed away by the perfect blood of Yeshua. It is how we keep ourselves unstained by the world.

In this new day, it is imperative to learn Him, press into His presence, and enter the Word. Entering into His Word with complete vulnerability enables union and will completely transform prayer. It is necessary to move His Beloved from intercession power to resurrection power, from a vague vision to fully seeing. We know and prophesy in part; when the perfect comes, the partial will be done away with (see 1 Cor. 13:10).

That evening, I had beckoned the Lord to heal me a little more from the pain I could no longer bear and opinions I did not want to own. He responded to my cries and answered me in the hiding place of thunder. This time, instead of merely pleading for the breakthrough, I responded to pain by diving into the Word, uninhibited and fully committed to His design. I recognized the clarity and soundness gifted as a result of visiting the spirit of knowledge realm. I understood His Word more completely than I did before. Abundant expressions of the revelations imparted during this venture have unfolded over time.

The spirit of knowledge will continue to bring a revelation of the reverential fear of the Lord. In the throne room, awe is continuously inspired. All of Heaven sings praises to His name, and out from the throne come flashes of lightning and peals of thunder. And there are seven lamps of fire burning before the throne, which are the sevenfold spirits of God (see Rev. 4:5).

We have a holy desire to know the deep mysteries of God and draw from His sevenfold spirit, accessible through the Word. The Beloved is growing up into all aspects into Him who is the Head, attaining to the unity of the faith and the knowledge of the Son (see Eph. 4:13). The revelation of true knowledge will bring forth mature sons who will perform mighty exploits in His name.

In this new era, a remnant will respond to the call of thunder and go into the Word of God. They will introduce the coming age, inspiring an end-time harvest. There will be an increase in the reverential fear of the

Lord as they draw from the eternal realm of the Spirit of the Lord.

When His voice is heard, there will be an electric display of splendor. A power will transform His Beloved. It is with expectation and holy fear that we long to hear His majestic voice thunder, shaking Heaven and earth, for He does not restrain the lightnings when His voice is heard. It will be the spirit of knowledge manifested at a corporate level, wondrous accounts of power surpassing understanding (see Job 37:4-5).

Chapter 2

The Reverential Fear of the Lord

The realm of the spirit of knowledge drew me into submission and strengthened my inner man. In the eternal space of His Spirit I am both hyperaware and consciously silenced at the same time. I understood that this was not only a revelation but a transformation. After the encounter, I reconnected with the realm of time and the atmosphere around me; I was carefully observant, examining my own being. My opinions and senses returned to me, and woven into every thought was an unending beckoning into reverence. I could feel His consuming fire expanding my capacity to believe, inspiring awe within me.

The spirit of knowledge is filled with myriads of light rays—each infinite, piercing as to the division of spirit and soul. Each beam of energy is an impartation accessible through the reverential fear of the Lord.

I am compelled to be experientially known by Him and to be transformed by a complete revelation of the reverential fear of the Lord. I struggle to honestly understand the magnitude of such a revelation, though I desire it more than ever before.

The prophet Isaiah's description of the seven spirits of God appears to directly connect the spirit of knowledge and the reverential fear of the Lord.

> *The Spirit of the Lord will rest on Him, the spirit of wisdom and understanding, the spirit of counsel and strength, the spirit of knowledge and the fear of the Lord* (Isaiah 11:2).

The spirit of truth imparted His delight into my very being so that I would dwell in the resting place of His glory forever, encountering deeper realms and greater lengths of awe. I desire to revere Him higher and wider with each passing moment and never revere Him less than I do right now. He is the God of wonder, majestic and complete; reverence is His design, His perfect delight.

> *And He will delight in the fear of the Lord* (Isaiah 11:3).

I have found that reverence and awe are our access to the deeper mysteries of His heart. We are growing a more significant curiosity about what is hidden in the depths. The Lord has stored up treasures, secrets, and thunders to be released to a certain generation. I believe they are stored up for the mature sons of God. These secrets are concealed until the fullness of time comes when a remnant reveres Him and yields to His design.

Yielding ourselves into conformity with His Word will reveal greater dimensions of awe and treasures unimaginable. The pure, love-infused prophetic word unified with the reverential fear of the Lord will catapult us into a time in history when a chosen generation will finally taste the powers of the coming age. His Beloved will present herself as royalty and lavish Him with honest worship. This awe-inspired worship will give access to secret places.

He has mysteries, powers, and wisdoms sealed up in His treasuries, designs that will captivate the masses and make the wisdom of the world look foolish. There is a remnant, complete in courage, that will access the storehouses and taste of His treasures. These mysteries are not for the arrogant or the foolish, for they will be humbly tasted by the reverent. Awe is our access. Awe is His treasure.

> [Yahweh] *is exalted, for He dwells on high; He has filled Zion with justice and righteousness. And* [Yahweh] *will be the stability of your times, a wealth of salvation, wisdom and knowledge; the fear of the Lord is His treasure* (Isaiah 33:5-6).

The fear of the Lord—a great privilege bestowed upon us.

A revelation of reverence is available for His Beloved. It is a gift, an object of affection from the Most High presented to us. Of its portions are life and peace; its essence is awe. The affectionate ones of this new era are longing for perfect union. They will position themselves to finally abide. True fellowship will be recognized by His righteousness and the reverence shining from their inner being. It is a perfect expression of the heart of a lover. Those immersed in reverential fear will touch union with God. It is not only His treasure but a gift He has bestowed upon us.

One True Revival

Several years ago, a messenger appeared to me in a vivid dream, giving me two special gifts. This was a strategic dream from the Lord with many important parts. I was in a large home that appeared to be my home; the messenger called it "love's home." Love's home is spacious and full. I was studying books that were piled high around me. I was on a couch, cozy and covered by blankets, notepads, books, and writing utensils. I had been studying alone in this space for a long time. A messenger of the Lord came to get me and gently directed me to another room. I was not prepared to leave my space; however, I recognized that it was imperative I see what was being revealed to me. Feeling the beckon of the

Lord drawing my heart to come out of hiding, I followed the messenger to a beautiful room where I received a revelation of love.

There are many rooms in love's house. During the journey to the new quarters, I recognized areas yet unexplored, several places I had never seen. I peeked through, trying to absorb all that I could as I walked past those rooms, locking away in my memories all that was tangible. The lights were off, so I could not grab much with my senses, but I knew that I would explore them one day and even live in their midst. I understood that each space was another revelation of love. Eventually, those lights will be turned on, and I will experience those rooms. For now, I will journey in the realms of love conveyed to me in this hour.

I knew I had traveled to this space before. Yet somehow, I was about to learn its depths for the very first time. It is as though my spirit had agreed to it long ago. I know I had been chosen for this love before the foundation of the world:

> *Blessed be the God and Father of our Lord Jesus Christ, who has blessed us with every spiritual blessing in the heavenly places in Christ, just as He chose us in Him before the foundation of the world, that we would be holy and blameless before Him. In love He predestined us to adoption as sons through Jesus Christ to Himself, according to the kind intention of*

> *His will, to the praise of the glory of His grace, which He freely bestowed on us in the Beloved.* (Ephesians 1:3-6).

As we walked through the passing on the way to my new revelation, the visitor pointed out messages that I would need on my journey, even things I had written somewhere in history or perhaps in the future. I had no memory of writing them, nor did I need one; love's house is not bound by time. God is love. God is eternal.

I quickly agreed with what had been written. These messages encouraged the hope within me, for they were messages already marked on my heart. I followed the messenger to the new dwelling place. I was awakened to the messages the moment I entered the room.

The fear I felt about the new journey was fading as I ventured further in.

I committed to the revelation. The new room's lights were turned on just as the messenger left. Each time the light in a room is turned on, it is symbolic of the revelation of love I am receiving. I was shocked to see that I was not alone in the room. It took me some time to adjust to this new space because I had become accustomed to being alone in the previous room.

After a quick introduction to the one standing in the room, I understood what the Lord was revealing to me. This is my future, my family, my love. I knew instantly that I had learned all I could in the previous room.

Bravely, I embraced the new day. I could feel myself becoming more vulnerable. The Lord had chosen for me. He had chosen the perfect story. I knew I would sway to a song that only Heaven knows and move into my destiny courageously.

Many beautiful things happened in this room, but my favorite moment is when I began to dance with the one my soul loves and step into the very rhythms of Heaven. This part of love's house drew me into courage and revealed union and intimacy.

The messenger showed many things that would take place both personally and corporately. I hid these away in my heart. Many of these secrets have come to pass. I was given two matchsticks. These matchsticks were at least one foot long and two inches in diameter. I was given the authority to strike both matches in due season.

One match would burn up the past. I was encouraged that the time had come to strike that match and let it burn, setting ablaze the old ways, systems, and rhythms. No longer will we *"call to mind the former things, or ponder the things of the past. Behold,* [He] *will do something new, now it will spring forth"* (Isa. 43:18-19).

Eventually, I understood the power of the second matchstick. Once the fullness of time comes, the second match will be carried as a torch and light the way to the one true revival.

THE LIGHT OF SUBMISSION

Though this dream was very personal, I know that I was also representing His Beloved that will carry a torch in this new era. It is the Lord's design that these two matchsticks serve their purpose. Certain leaders or torchbearers will be given the great responsibility of striking the match and carrying the torch. The courageous, reverent lovers will lead this march.

The first matchstick burned up the past, the old ways that do not work. These old religious systems are without reverence. They. Are. Dead. The Lord has already been burning up these old ways. Though many will try to resurrect what God has destroyed, these old wicked systems have no life and no lasting fruit. They will not be resurrected.

However, the second matchstick is one of resurrection power; when lit, it will light the way to the one true revival. It will be as a torch that lights the path for the forerunners carrying love's purpose; it will also be the flame that initiates a full-blown fire of the Spirit. The light of that matchstick is submission.

Yielding up our spirit is His perfect design. Having suffered excruciating pain, Jesus hung on the cross carrying within Him the power to stop it all in a moment. The One who is fully God and perfect majesty, Creator of the universe, chose instead to yield up His Spirit. This was the final demonstration on earth before the resurrection. Matthew 27:49 says that the mockers were hollering, "Let us see whether Elijah will come to save Him." Still, Jesus followed the Father's perfect design, submitting fully to His ways.

> *And Jesus cried out again with a loud voice, and yielded up His spirit. And behold, the veil of the temple was torn in two from top to bottom; and the earth shook and the rocks were split* (Matthew 27:50-51).

The blood of Jesus is the very light of submission. We are receiving a greater revelation of the blood. There is a spirit of freedom available that will urge a congregation of people to ponder the power of "the yield." Beyond the mere thought, the torchbearers will begin to move in submission, and the colors of this freedom will radiate within her. The remnant will be imbued with His light and go into His Word, yielding up her opinions, concepts, and mindsets. I believe these sons of God are on the earth now and will carry this torch and light the way to the one true revival.

The light of the flame is a great mystery that the historical heroes of the faith experienced—the beautiful mystery of yielding their will to the will of the Father. Just as the cloud of witnesses understood and touched the power of future days, so will a remnant of God's people. They will carry this mysterious torch, which will further inspire submission. The reverential fear of the Lord is our access to a greater level of awe, and it will bring forth the revelation of this mystery.

"The one who says he abides in Him ought himself to walk in the same manner as He walked" (1 John 2:6)—perfecting the love of God in Him. The reverent will carry the second matchstick, and submission will be the declaration of their walk. They will abide in Him. The flame within that fire will brand the hearts of the lonely, calling them into their destiny. More than a simple light shining in the night, the flame of submission carries a message of hope, union, life, and peace.

VULNERABLE

The realm of the spirit of knowledge transformed my thoughts and opinions, even giving me a greater understanding of previous encounters. I can look back at visitations such as love's home and understand more completely. Pondering the memory, I recognize similar themes that I had not originally grasped.

One of these important revelations is submission. I did not realize how difficult it was for me to leave my original room in love's home. I truly had to lay down the old way to pursue what God had in store. The vulnerability was not easy for me. As I refer back to the revelation of love's home, I recognize the reverential fear of the Lord had been teaching me to yield to His design.

In the spirit of knowledge, the reverential fear of the Lord increased within me. Eventually, the process of yielding, and entering into His knowledge became easier. I can recognize the message of submission when I think back to previous encounters, though I had no word to describe it before encountering God's knowledge.

I have now experienced this process of yielding into His Spirit many times. I had another encounter a year after the experience with knowledge. I was able to dive into the yielding chamber, uninhibited. In this place, I saw His messenger standing in the garden waving for me to come in. This was another moment of beckoning me into transparency and vulnerability. I hesitated for only a moment, unsure because of my failures. My spirit remembered this place so completely, so I knew that my negative thoughts about myself were unnecessary. The only thing that mattered was His thoughts toward me, so I dove in without restraint.

I believe it is a picture of what we can expect as we learn to touch a future day. Yielding will become easier, and we will know His thoughts. What a beautiful friendship with the Most High—to be known by Him, yield to Him, and revere Him.

There is rest in this abiding. I have found that I have greater confidence in vulnerability with God in the weeks, months, and years following the encounter with God's knowledge. I recognized a quietude in my inner man that I never knew before. I heard the Lord's words in my spirit: "In quietness, the reverent will know Me."

The one who joins himself to the Lord is one spirit with Him (1 Corinthians 6:17).

Reverential Fear

He has made an everlasting covenant with us, one of life and peace, and He gave them as an object of reverence so we will revere Him and stand in awe of His name (see Mal. 2:5). He puts the fear of the Lord in our hearts so that we will not turn away from Him (see Jer. 32:40). It is both a love gift and our great honor. Reverence is an everlasting verse in love's song.

A remnant of God's people will experience the full measure of love. Ephesians 3 describes love as this incomprehensible reality that surpasses human knowledge, with vast measurements even into eternity.

Reverence has lengths and widths the same way, for it is massive in exploration. I have seen this reverence, these immovable parts of love, like an ocean with depths engulfing me in submission. I have seen that place where the ocean meets the sky, and soaring to its heights is without burden.

It is power without measure. This kind of earth-shaking love and awe will surely prepare the Bride for her groom's coming. Intimacy is available for the awe-inspired Bride who will yield at His command. The Beloved will call to Him with her soul laid bare, and He will pursue her with the whispers of His lips and the thunders of His heart.

CHAPTER 3

CIVIL WAR AND THE SURVEYORS

Look unto the heavens and see; and survey the skies: they are higher than thou.
—JOB 35:5 DARBY

THE CIVIL WAR

The civil war in the land drew the attention of the entire world. They were battling over agendas such as abortion, sex trafficking, political corruption, race, and pride. The list goes on. Even professed Christians took their gaze off the Lord and engaged in wicked plots against humanity. Theological debates began to separate ministries and confuse the people. There were divisions of all kinds. This separation will continue to go on until the Lord returns.

I saw this civil war prophetically long before it started. Before the fires, the storms, the protests, the virus, the political upheaval, I was alerted that everything was about to change. Not only would there be horrific pain in the land, but 2020 would also be a great opportunity for the Lord's people to come up higher. In the middle of all the separation, the Lord is raising up a community that will shine in the darkest night.

God granted me access to multiple visionary encounters that warned of future warfare. Not only did these encounters expose wickedness, but they also revealed the victorious rise of the eagles. These eagles will look up higher above the turmoil on the land. They will learn to fly. The Lord will give them tools to bring people out of darkness.

One of the dreams I received was so real that I must explain it as a memory lived and not a vision seen. Here is that dream:

> My husband, the children, and I were driving away from the horrors of the civil war on the land. As we journeyed away, we recognized that we had a fading curiosity of the war's demise. We were very aware that revival was coming. All of creation was longing, waiting eagerly for the revealing of the sons of God. Regardless of the wickedness manifesting before our eyes, we knew there was an

increase of faith and courage accessible to the soaring ones.

We were driving away from the chaos. We were driving by faith to a new place. We were uncertain where we were going. As we were driving, it appeared to us that a wall as high as the sky blocked our path. The war still in our peripheral, we were hollering to the Lord with questions of every kind, uncertain if we would find a land of freedom. It appeared that there was nowhere left to go. The wall was too quickly in our path; plots to move, blow up, or knock it down did not appear to be an option. The only option available seemed ill-fitting for such a predicament; even so, we heard the Lord speak:

"Just go up."

The anxiety on the land behind us grew distant as we drove straight up the wall. In great courage, we yielded into God's design. Identifying Heaven's plan to take us higher was exhilarating. Outside the car window, we watched two eagles manifest, wing to wing. They held hands, soaring without restraint above the chaos and away from the war. I understood these eagles were a symbolic representation of the soaring ones who carry the flying eagle anointing. My spirit leaped with anticipation as I heard these words:

> "It is the time of the eagle! It is the time of the eagle!"
>
> I felt the excitement for this new day rising within me. The two eagles flying together represented unity. We are better together.

The eagles are symbolic of a remnant of the Lord's people who will introduce the coming age, the age when the infilling of God never ends. Previous eras were qualified by certain things, but the coming age will be qualified by the fullness of the knowledge of God. The eagles will understand the necessity of the Spirit more fully. They are ensouled beings who will draw from realms unseen, filling their soul to the fullness, into every member. There are realms of His Spirit that human language cannot define, nor soul alone can stand before. There are realms only interpreted in awe and expressed through reverent submission. A representation of the pure prophetic will emerge; they will be a true voice for the Lord. It is the time of the eagle to come up higher and introduce the coming age.

> *After these things I looked, and behold, a door standing open in heaven, and the first voice which I had heard, like the sound of a trumpet speaking with me, said, "Come up here, and I will show you what must take place after these things." Immediately I was in the Spirit; and*

> *behold, a throne was standing in heaven, and One sitting on the throne* (Revelation 4:1-2).

Until the Lord returns, there will continue to be torment and chaos in the land. But though the deep darkness has risen in the land, so will a bright light. The Lord will bring in His harvest. We are in the end. It is time we know what the Lord has to say about this day and how to equip His people to bring in this harvest.

Throughout this experience, the Lord encouraged us to go up and to look up. As we did, He showed us what will take place and how to posture ourselves in the final hours before His return.

I kept my gaze continually on the signs in the sky. The clouds were forming into various shapes resembling tools. I looked closer, trying to identify with my eyes. While my husband, Paul Keith, was still driving up higher, I engaged my spirit and submitted to the revelation.

Submitting to the revelation is an essential part of receiving from His Spirit. Truth is not always easy. Even when it is easy to receive, our own opinions block the fullness of the revelation. We must engage with our spirit so that we can receive full impartation.

I obediently submitted myself into true knowledge as the message from Heaven invited me in. I was uncertain at first why I was seeing what I was seeing; I leaned in closer to get a better look. As I did I was filled with hope for the coming days.

The distraction of the civil war no longer tugged at my wonderment, for I was reading Heaven's plans, captivated by divine design. I fixed my eyes intently on the skies and recognized curious tools in the distance overhead. Tools with which I was not familiar.

As I leaned into the revelations, I identified that they were surveying tools, spiritual devices that would begin to build the new day and prepare a place to equip the coming harvest.

While I was looking in the sky at these tools, the Lord spoke to me, and I listened:

"You are a surveyor."

In this experience I am symbolic of a remnant of people who are considered surveyors. As I continued to grow into understanding, I learned who these surveyors are and what they will do. I will explain more about these surveyors, but first, I will conclude the dream.

I assume we made it to safety. After all, the wall was not a real obstacle, and the civil war was not our battle. We captured the message from the Lord and embraced the truth. If it were not for the civil war and the wall, we would not have left the land of fear to pursue the heights of freedom. We would not have had the opportunity to experience the miracle of going up and escaping against all odds.

THE SURVEYORS

The surveyors will introduce the coming age. As I have mentioned many times, there is a harvest that we must gather. We have entered a new era. This era will see the fulfillment of this prophetic promise. This harvest will need a safe place to heal and execute their dreams. The surveyors will identify and sometimes build places of influence that will help guide the Lord's people. These will be homes of refuge, healing, and spiritual growth. Each community will be administrated by leadership anointed and ordained by God. The surveyors are currently identifying this leadership and gathering the harvesters.

These communities will be built from heavenly design. The surveyors will not follow an old pattern but patterns found in the Spirit of the Lord; they will access the seven lamps of fire, which are the seven spirits of God. They are currently identifying the harvesters, assessing the land, and determining where to build.

The surveyors will be assigned to designated areas. In some occasions the areas of influence will come from an alliance of three or more regions functioning and learning together. They will access the mysteries of God and build according to the Spirit. These alliances will be equipped to build people and build unity in relationships.

A portal of ingenuity and creativity will flood the coming days with ideas, inventions, technology, and communication. This outpouring will touch both the harvesters and the harvest. These curious places of influence will help guide the Lord's people in the ways of this new era.

The Lord will give surveying tools to those who can be trusted. They will build safe places for people to dream, heal, and become mature sons of God. The Lord has taught me the importance of being a safe place for as long as I can remember. It was recited to me like this many years ago:

> Be like Philemon.
> Be the one that encourages the remnant,
> The chosen, the downcast and broken;
> The writers and singers and dancers and dreamers;
> The lively, the tired, inventors and flyers;
> Comfort them, exhort them, and refresh them.

Philemon was a safe place.

> *For I have come to have much joy and comfort in your love, because the hearts of the saints have been refreshed through you, brother* (Philemon 1:7).

Knit Together in Love

Those in tune with His Spirit will learn to communicate by supernatural brilliance across the earth and relationships will be formed through realms unseen. These relationships will not be strengthened by natural memories alone but formed by unity built in the Spirit.

In transparency, God's people will unite and become encouraged in the ways of communion. As they are intimately acquainted with the One who is love, their hearts will be knit together, resulting in a true knowledge of God's mystery.

> *That their hearts may be encouraged, having been knit together in love, and attaining to all the wealth that comes from the full assurance of understanding, resulting in a true knowledge of God's mystery, that is, Christ Himself, in whom are hidden all the treasures of wisdom and knowledge* (Colossians 2:2-3).

Take Your Seat at the Table

By God's foreknowledge He chose and set apart a Bride whose character is not stained by religious nonsense nor consumed by greed and selfish ambition; without spot or wrinkle she will represent His heart. The Bride will receive a revelation of God's nature and light, dismissing the old ways and religious systems, coming to the true knowledge of who He is. She will yield into a perfect design, attaining to the unity of the faith and the true knowledge of God. This submission will be a radiant display of her worth.

All of the Lord's people will learn their worth; it is a necessary revelation in the days ahead. I experienced the Lord's table years ago, where I received a proper understanding of my value.

I was in a deep revelatory state that felt real to all of my senses. I was standing over the Lord's table. His chosen had come to dine and partake of His tender mercies. I was encouraged by a woman of great stature in the Spirit that I should sit and dine with them at His table. I was hesitant to take my seat. While I pondered the idea, I took notice of the peculiar design. Its shape is not like an average table.

The table of the Lord was both inviting and dreadful. I did not know any of the people seated in the natural, but I knew them in the realm of the spirit. I understood they were highest royalty. I looked around the room finding somewhere else to sit that would be more suitable. I did not yet know my worth and thought that I did not belong there. I set my standards low regarding who I would accompany. As I quickly tried to dismiss the invitation, this humble yet very prominent woman urged me to take my seat at His table.

A chair miraculously appeared from another realm. It was a chair prepared for me. As I sat, I quickly learned that everybody at the table teaches and everybody at the table learns. Once I took my seat at the table I understood my value. I am royalty.

In this experience, I am symbolic of the Beloved of the Lord. The woman who invited me to the table is a representation of a surveyor, one who identifies and gathers.

In the atmosphere of honor, some who are disillusioned will learn their value, not found in flattery or selfish ambition, but established in true honor and the reverential fear of the Lord. The manifested presence of perfect love will bring forth blessings that will draw the broken and lonely to His table.

This word *honor* means "a value, a price, perceived worth."

When honor is present people learn their worth and step into the full measure of their calling. The destructive words and memories from the past melt away and no longer have the authority to frame our thinking. In this place, we *"put on the new self who is being renewed to a true knowledge according to the image of the One who created him"* (Col. 3:10).

In this atmosphere, we learn who we are.

Divinely Powerful

> *And He gave some as apostles, and some as prophets, and some as evangelists, and some as pastors and teachers, for the equipping of the saints for the work of service, to the building up*

> *of the body of Christ; until we all attain to the unity of the faith, and of the knowledge of the Son of God, to a mature man, to the measure of the stature which belongs to the fullness of Christ* (Ephesians 4:11-13).

Anything standing against that true knowledge is an attempt to affect time. Ultimately it is an attempt to delay the Bride from reaching her destination.

I must point out—the knowledge of God is our timeline.

Imagine drawing a timeline out on a piece of paper using life events only—memories of pain, sorrow, laughter, mistakes, enjoyment. Do not label the timeline with years, months, or weeks. Now remove the emotional memories from the timeline and imagine filling the timeline with only moments of transformation that bring you from glory to glory into the image of God. Upon reaching the fullness of time, the result would be the unity of the faith and the true knowledge of the Son of God.

Let's pay close attention to the language recorded in Daniel 12:3-4.

> *Those who have insight will shine brightly like the brightness of the expanse of heaven, and those who lead the many to righteousness, like the stars forever and ever. But as for you, Daniel, conceal these words and seal up the book until the end of time; many will go back and forth, and knowledge will increase.*

The people will go to and fro in the land, witnessing of the testimonies of Yeshua; however, this back and forth is not limited to the work on the earth. Many will go back and forth into the realm of the Spirit. They will experience the Lord, ascending and descending as though through a window or a portal. Through these encounters, the Bride will grow into the unity of the faith and the true knowledge of God.

There are forces of evil set up against the Lord's Beloved. The mission of these evil powers is to stop the Bride from reaching her destination. Those who are divinely powerful will defeat the power of delay. To be divinely powerful means more than healing the sick and moving in signs and wonders. To be divinely powerful is to protect the word of truth.

> *For the weapons of our warfare are not of the flesh, but divinely powerful for the destruction of fortresses. We are destroying speculations and every lofty thing raised up against the knowledge of God, and we are taking every thought captive to the obedience of Christ, and we are ready to punish all disobedience, whenever your obedience is complete* (2 Corinthians 10:4-6).

False doctrine is an example of a lofty thing raised up against the knowledge of God. This word *lofty* means "presumptuous; to exalt itself in arrogance; the act of taking something to be true or adopting a particular attitude or behavior."

The behaviors we adopt that God does not ordain are in all actuality set up against His timeline and affect the process of maturity. The maturation process happens as the Lord's Beloved grows into true knowledge and we learn to move in new patterns and completely abandon an old format.

> *As a result* [of true knowledge], *we are no longer to be children, tossed here and there by waves and carried about by every wind of doctrine, by the trickery of men, by craftiness in deceitful scheming; but speaking the truth in love, we are to grow up in all aspects into Him who is the head, even Christ* (Ephesians 4:14-15).

Sadly, in this hour, many will be deceived. False prophets will continue to rise, and many will follow after their leadership. These corrupt leaders operate from another spirit, a false spirit. They will lead many astray into delusions, filling their heads with fantasies and impossible agendas. These lofty imaginations are an example of a fortress or stronghold set up against the knowledge of God. This is the enemy's ploy to cause delay.

The Lord has provided a people who will come against these wicked agendas in reverence of the truth. The surveyors are of those who are divinely powerful for the destruction of these strongholds. They have a massive job both corporately and individually to encourage the tearing down of fortresses and help remove the restraints that previously contributed to this delay.

A divinely powerful person is a protector of the truth. We love powerful displays of His Spirit including miracles, healings, signs, and wonders. The definition of a divinely powerful person as described in 2 Corinthians 10:4 is one who fights for the truth. This includes the truth about who He is and who we are. It includes the truth about the mysteries of Heaven and what future days will look like.

The Language of Light

The new day's architectural design will introduce Heaven's perspective but not only through natural places of refuge. The design of the Spirit is not limited to one type of tangible expression; even more, it is a spiritual connection that defines union to a divided people. By His Spirit He will encourage His Beloved into beautiful expressions of unity, inspiring a great harvest.

This is what we are building in the new day—a mature people who will journey in the true light, which enlightens every man. For *"as many as received Him, to them He gave the right to become children of God"* (John 1:12).

Those who will be birthed in this new day will understand this light and move mightily in its curious design.

We have a treasure in earthen vessels. His name is Light—a radiance that fills us as we are experientially known by Him. Glory, evoking the perfect opinion, for He has shone in our hearts to give the light of the knowledge of the glory of God in the face of Christ. This light is the optimal form of communication in the new day. Light communication will eradicate miscommunication and bring a common opinion and a beautiful union to the Lord's Beloved. Shining in the light of His glory, they will rise in the darkness, and let not their heart feel hopeless. This radiance is a response to the message from the prophet Isaiah:

> *Arise, shine; for your light has come, and the glory of the Lord has risen upon you. For behold, darkness will cover the earth and deep darkness the peoples; but the Lord will rise upon you and His glory will appear upon you. Nations will come to your light, and kings to the brightness of your rising. Lift up your eyes round about and see; they all gather together, they come to you. Your sons will come from afar, and your daughters will be carried in the arms. Then you will see and be radiant, and your heart will thrill and rejoice; because the abundance of the sea will be turned to you. ... They will go up with acceptance on My altar, and I shall glorify My glorious house* (Isaiah 60:1-5,7).

Reverential fear, holy affection, and courage will pull the new era into dimensions of light that have rarely been accessed. They will carry an aroma of holy radiance that will captivate the masses. As the light of the world, it is their great privilege to shine before men in such a way that they glorify the Father in Heaven. By virtue of the seven spirits of God, they will shine like the brightness of the expanse of Heaven and lead the many to righteousness.

This article written by Paul Keith describes this pure light of Heaven and its impact on the Beloved:

> The pure white light of Heaven will proceed from the throne to be imparted into the spirit and soul of the Lord's people to make us divine carriers of His virtue. Many will encounter the lights of Heaven in private worship and in corporate settings in amplified ways over the coming months and years. This light will manifest as the sevenfold spirit of God in the same way that pure white light directed through a prism highlights the seven colors of the spectrum.
>
> It pleases the Lord for us to embody His light. When we lead the life as one "native-born" to the light, we enjoy the fruit or effect of that light consisting of kindness, uprightness of heart and truth. This is the day that individuals will begin to walk in the light of revelation they possess.

> There must be an experiential quality to our walk with the Lord. Not only do we experience Him in a tangible way, but also in practical ways that exude the spiritual light that has been deposited within us.
>
> This is the model for the lost to be drawn to the Kingdom of Light; then the masses will be drawn to our light and fulfill the prophecies of Daniel when he said, "Those who have insight will shine brightly like the brightness of the expanse of heaven, and those who lead the many to righteousness, like the stars forever and ever" (Daniel 12:3).
>
> We have now crossed a threshold into the place where we begin to do what we have for so long talked about. This is especially true in the Western Church. This is the day of lights or the day that people began to walk in the light of Heaven.

Compelled to express the light of Heaven, the remnant will tell the story of when the day got brighter. They will submit into the ways of union and the ways of His heart. The glimmer of this submission will dance across the darkest skies and paint the hills. They will be a demonstration of the glory of the Lord. It will be important to learn the ways of light, which could include having a "light" vocabulary. When we know something well, we can communicate and express it. We must have a language for light.

The distribution of light is a massive revelation; its reveal is something spectacular that we will see in the coming days. There are expressions of light the greatest scientists in history have not explored. In the latter days, a generation will see its depths in one bright display. This light will shine during the darkest hour.

Few have accessed this realm already. They are a prototype of the remnant who will understand light, sound, and time in the coming days.

Barry Stephen Goldfarb, a Messianic believer, is a super genius, light engineer, and inventor. Throughout his journey of teaching and learning about sight, scent, taste, touch, and sound, he has developed more than 175 polysensory inventions with dozens of patents to his credit. Goldfarb has a true appreciation for the Lord's artwork with a desire that His people would experience the display of His splendor through every sense simultaneously even as music is to our ears. He has a unique gift to understand and create in light, space, and time.

Below is an excerpt from an article that Goldfarb wrote entitled "The Substance of Light." in which he explains the connection between light and time. I believe a community of people that the Lord is gathering now will have a gift like Goldfarb to understand light. They will move in the authority of the Father of Lights. They will overtake the realms of darkness currently keeping us from coming into the fullness of time.

It is written: *"Eye has not seen, nor ear heard, nor have entered into the heart of man the things which God has prepared for those who love Him"* (1 Cor. 2:9 NKJV). There are mysteries promised by the Spirit. This generation has already witnessed inventions beyond most comprehension. The end-time remnant will even exceed what former generations have accessed and developed. Goldfarb has tapped into another realm and we can learn of the mysteries of light from his knowledge. The remnant of the last days will speak the language of light.

This is what Goldfarb has to say about light:

> Light as art is virtually at day one in its developmental stage. Up to the present we have depended on space for creating light art, and have (for the most part) used light and color as architectural elements.
>
> I believe the Lord our God would have us set free from convention by providing us the ability to suspend light, through no apparent means, in free space, as a three and four dimensional hovering sculpture made of light. This light will be capable of creating space and time, in a similar way as sound does with music.
>
> If art is "spirit made tangible" then light art should be able to take us somewhere else; somewhere deeper where we've never been

> before... Not for us to self-indulge in a new sensual experience, but to break chains, free prisoners, and bring good news to those who are perishing; and to do so by way of a powerful, hitherto unknown vocabulary of light, that His Light may be clearly seen and understood.[1]

We are praying now for a light vocabulary. According to Goldfarb, this suspended light is capable of creating *and* shaping space *and* time. Perhaps this mystery will help destroy the power of delay. Divinely powerful people will be able to maneuver through time. It is a key to bringing the Body of Christ into the fullness. To gain a comprehension of the dimension of light will enable us to fulfill our destiny to shine in the darkness in such a way that the darkness cannot comprehend it. For:

> *In the beginning was the Word, and the Word was with God, and the Word was God. ...In Him was life, and the life was the Light of men. The Light shines in the darkness, and the darkness did not comprehend it* (John 1:1,4-5).

Cloud of Witnesses

This will be the age of the rise of the Bride, who will soon move as a unified force, accessing more than the heroes of the faith who had gone before us and gained approval but have not yet received the promise.

There is a beautiful list of faithful heroes who have begun to pave the way in wisdom and revelation. Each has lived approved and strategically defined lives. Our unveiling as mature sons is directly connected to their story, where we see His glory expressed in every verse. The cloud of witnesses is a powerful encouragement to move us into union. They gained approval through their faith but did not receive what was promised because the Lord provided something better for us. We will be made perfect together (see Heb. 11).

It is not limited to the heroes mentioned in Scripture. There are many faithful forerunners who created a launching pad for the remnant in these last days. These courageous leaders gained wisdom and revelation, not by their experience in the "business" of ministry but by their experience in communion with God.

Each of these forerunners has ascended the mountain of the Lord. I have seen the great mountain of faith in a visionary encounter many years ago. It is both beautiful and conflicting. The splendors of the highlands were formed out of trial. The colors of the hills were marked in courage by those who have gone before us. They have left their color as a map to keep us in the ways of truth.

In a supernatural experience I was ascending this mountain. My legs were heavy with burden; fatigue was desperate to pull me under its deception. I heard the blasts of sorrow and trouble from down below, much like the sounds of the civil war. Despite the struggle to go on,

I pursued higher elevation. Motivated by wisdom and understanding, I quickly recognized the value of courage. It is my reward. Disconnecting from the blasts of sorrow and trouble attempting to silence my bravery, I understood I must ascend as one of great valor. I made the mindful decision that this heart will not feel hopeless, for by design the mountain of faith caused the heroes before me to be heavy in praise! For He has overcome the world!

As I pressed on in my journey, I heard these words: "Who will ascend the mountain of faith? Few have gone there. For that mountain is strong and some legs are weak. Since we are surrounded by so great a cloud of witnesses, let us also lay aside every weight, and sin which clings so closely, and let us run with endurance the race that is set before us" (see Heb. 12:1).

I overcame and continued to pursue the heights. I saw that those who had gone before me had left their color painted on the hills of Zion. These are colors only seen in realms of faith—beautiful and strategic designs. Each color represents wisdom attained by faith. Together displaying a common opinion as guidelines for the Body of Christ. There are glory colors still to be revealed from Heaven. Colors of this new era that will complete the artistry on Zion. These colors are the manifold wisdom of God.

> *To bring to light what is the administration of the mystery which for ages has been hidden in God who created all things; so that the manifold*

> *wisdom of God might now be made known* (Ephesians 3:9-10).

He created all things in order to display and make known His manifold wisdom. One definition of the word *manifold* is "marked with a great variety of colors."

Those who ascend the mountain each carry a portion of revelation and share it with the Body of Christ. This is demonstrated in my dream by the cloud of witnesses who left their display of His splendor on the hills. I felt them pulling on this generation to complete our portion so that they might be made perfect. Regardless of trial and adversity, our faithful heroes painted Zion and creatively expressed His wisdom, stamping the mountain with its depth.

In servile manner, a remnant will pursue the mountain and access a perfect measure of wisdom. This opinion is absent of fear and fully motivated by love. Speaking wisdom among those who are mature, the remnant will pursue these hidden mysteries. They will talk a wisdom not of this age nor of the rulers of this age who are passing away; they will speak God's wisdom in a mystery, the hidden wisdom which God predestined before the ages to our glory (see 1 Cor. 2).

BLUEPRINTS

There is a vast glory and eternal revelation that will form our opinion from the wisdom of another realm. This opinion is God's opinion, and it is how we will build the new day. The surveyors are positioned with the Lord to receive the new model's blueprints, which is the new day. The new format will not be found in former agendas; it is only found in the heart of God. What is built will not come from mythical ideas formed in the thoughts of a man nor orchestrated by human agenda. These plans will bring the Body of Christ into the unity of the faith and the true knowledge of God.

The surveyors have a part in gathering the people to complete God's perfect design. They will align and connect the messages from past and present. Those whom they gather will be a community of harvesters who will express His heart and bring in a harvest—people who are fully light, for they are the children of the Father of Lights with whom there is no variation or shifting shadow, brought forth by the word of truth (see James 1:17-18).

Note

1. Barry Stephen Goldfarb, "Substance of Light," WhiteDove Ministries Newsletter, 2002.

CHAPTER 4

TETHERED

In this new era, a generation will operate from the resting place of His might. This resting place is found in abiding. There is a direct connection between intimacy and power. I learned this truth in an encounter I had with the spirit of might. Distinct from my experience with the spirit of knowledge, the spirit of might drew me into a deeper understanding of the places stamped by God. I will share this encounter and explain the revelation of truth I received.

I had just come out of another experience, which I will share later. Some might describe it as a deep state of consciousness, but it felt as though I was returning from another dimension and coming back to the realm of time. I quickly recalled everything from the previous experience before being drawn back in quickly. I felt a heavy weight come over me like a blanket as His Spirit lulled me into another dimension—the realm of the spirit of might.

I looked out into the expanse, and there I saw a massive explosion. Power, light, electricity surging from its demeanor, the spirit of might blasted across the heavens. His heart painted across the skies of eternity a perfect song of grace corralled by unrelenting fire. His design brushed every inch of existence. I relished in contentment as the spirit of might permeated my being, taking me layers deep in rest. My body and soul continued to decompress as I yielded up my spirit, ascending into a new dimension, a cosmic world.

The cosmos's expanse is lavished with beauty and colors not yet revealed on the earth—colors found in the depths of the rainbow and the core of fire's flame. Colors eye has not seen in the land. The spirit of might burns through the heavens.

El Gibbor reigns in the heavenliness, extending His authority through massive rays of light that touch every frame. He is infinitely generous in space and authority. The Word of God operates eternally in the realm of His Spirit—Yeshua, the full expression of the sevenfold spirit of God.

I could feel the heat of burning light imparting a word of correction that transformed my thoughts and the motivation of my heart:

> Rest is not something to be done when you are empty. It is a fullness to operate from to demonstrate My power.

This reality awakened me to the truth about the power of rest and the freedom found in the boundaries of His Spirit. I began to grasp the reality that the spirit of might gave me the ability to pause. At that moment I recognized freedom from disturbance. I found quietude in His might. This is an important part of submission. It is a glorious exchange submitting my worry and receiving His might. He continues to do for the Beloved in His strength what we could never achieve on our own.

It was clear to me that I am given a certain amount of authority and an allotment of time to execute that authority on the earth. The authority I operate in is due in part to my ability to find this resting place. The greater the rest, the greater the power. This is an example of the spirit of might's demonstration in the realm of time. It is His story told through His Beloved.

In humility, a remnant will operate in full authority and learn the resting place of might. The Spirit of God will ignite in His Beloved a fire that will light the way to the one true revival. The revelation of eternity will burn within her as a light that shines in the darkest hour.

The spirit of might is a protector, dynamic yet elegant, explosive, and calming. He is justice, and He is mercy. The One who measured the waters in the hollow of His hand comes as might with His recompense before Him; however, like a shepherd, He will gently tend to His flock and carry them close to His heart (see Isa. 40). He will manifest His might not only as a ruling arm but as the One who will gather His lambs and minister His rest.

I felt awestruck wonder as I elegantly danced through His creation in my allotted space. I understood that we are created with a desire to be a part of a story, a part of a dance. Many will spend a lifetime pursuing that story through striving and selfish ambition but never actually come to the fulfillment of a romance well lived and well told. His story is in the eternal place of His might, and it touches the lengths and the widths, strong and unending. I felt His story as I moved through this realm. I saw His Word written in the blast of His Spirit. It touches every crevice with perfect peace.

The Womb of Understanding

The Lord's design is that we would know Him and be known by Him. Experiencing my Father is my greatest pleasure; each memory with Him changes me. I have come to learn that true revelation introduces transformation. Encountering might and learning the beauty of rest was profound. I am still in the process of submitting fully to this revelation.

As I mentioned, the Lord had been visiting me throughout that night, drawing me into rest. I first entered this rest during a visitation I had with Yeshua just before being drawn into the realm of might. The Lord came and shared the desire of His heart for His Beloved. A beautiful story of intimacy. This experience is not easy to express in understandable language. I hold it with great reverence. He imparted a message during our time together. It is a message of hope. It is a message of true knowledge.

He sat to my right, propped up higher than me, barefoot with beautiful, deep-golden skin. His hair hung just above His shoulders. The lover of my soul came during the night to abide with me, breaking through the weariness that had seemingly consumed every cell of my being. I needed Him to come to me as Constant Trust, Dependable Friend, and Perfect Lover. The Son came to me that night. He came, and He stayed awhile.

There was a fascinatingly romantic longing. I had to see His eyes more clearly and witness a sparkle between Him and me. Still, the seriousness of eyes like flames of fire cut like laser beams through my emotions, saturating my soul with truth.

Our communication was divine; He knew me, and I knew as much of Him as He was willing to share. I knew as much of Him as I was able to withstand. He is the fullest wisdom, the deepest understanding, and the most complex creativity.

We are connected by a ribbon. The ribbon is pearly white, with an iridescent hue, described by Solomon as a silver cord (see Eccles. 12:6). Surprisingly, it resembled a sea plant. It waved like plants wave in the waters of the sea. The ribbon of pearl hue came out of His being with several parts; a part was connected directly to my inner man, while others floated freely.

He sat on a wooden box comfortably. The atmosphere was neither air nor water. It was thick, perfect liquid, transparent, and even intelligent. Clearing my lungs and strengthening me with every breath. I was in a womb, the womb of understanding.

We were strongly connected by the ribbon that seemed to be an umbilical cord feeding me true knowledge, life, and rest. The ribbon of pearl is a conduit of the true knowledge of God. It carries its full message of life and reveals God's true knowledge to whom the Son wills and according to what the recipient can receive.

> *All things have been handed over to Me by My Father; and no one knows the Son except the Father; nor does anyone know the Father except the Son, and anyone to whom the Son wills to reveal Him. Come to Me, all who are weary and heavy-laden, and I will give you rest* (Matthew 11:27-28).

During my time with the Son, I was coming alive. It was as though I was growing in understanding as a baby would grow in a womb. I realized that I am tethered to Him, ever receiving an infilling of knowledge, prophecy, and life. I can endure the world's trials because I am tethered to the One who is perfect rest, hidden away with Christ to be revealed with Christ in His glory.

I am hidden away, being renewed to true knowledge, immersed in the wisdom of Yeshua. In this place, there is no pain, and perfect rest consumes me.

> *For you have died and your life is hidden with Christ in God. When Christ, who is our life, is revealed, then you also will be revealed with Him in glory. Therefore consider the members of your earthly body as dead to immorality, impurity, passion, evil desire, and greed, which amounts to idolatry. For it is because of these things that the wrath of God will come upon the sons of disobedience, and in them you also once walked, when you were living in them. But now you also, put them all aside...and have put on the new self who is being renewed to a true knowledge according to the image of the One who created him* (Colossians 3:3-8,10).

As I sat in His presence, I had no conscious thought of worry or fear. I did not bring a list of questions or prayer requests to submit to Him. In His presence, I did not have a single concern. I was complete in rest. I would have expected the eyes of the One who is perfect rest to be as the crystal seas, serene and translucent. I am certain His eyes glimmer like that too. It was the eyes like flames of fire that encountered me that evening.

I sat that night in the depths, connected to the lover of my soul by a spiritual cord I cannot adequately describe. With flames of fire, beautiful golden skin, and peace overwhelming, He fed me rest that went deep into my bones. He is rest, and He fed me from the fullness.

I was hidden away in a safe place with my greatest friend and truest love as He taught me mysteries that I was destined to learn at that moment. These mysteries will keep me eagerly traveling the narrow road regardless of the pain that I might encounter along the way. The enemies of God are constantly lurking around with a wicked desire to steal our rest and inflict pain not intended by the Lord. This pain has become an enemy to the process of maturity. The objective of this evil agenda is to come against the true knowledge of God. It is an attempt to delay. Many are trapped in pain and not responding to the definitive call to maturity. Because of this, many have built up a resistance to true knowledge.

There is a beckon from the Lord, drawing His Beloved into union with Him. As I grew in the womb of understanding, I responded to the call of maturity. This is symbolic of the Beloved who grows into the fullness of Christ. I know without a doubt, the delay will end, and His Beloved will attain to the unity of the faith and the knowledge of the Son of God to a mature man to the measure of the stature which belongs to the fullness of Christ.

Let's Talk About Pain

As I sat with the Son, He opened my eyes to the truth about delay and its connection to buried pain. His

Beloved is currently resisting the true knowledge of God. Many people encountered pain along the narrow way, pain that was too difficult to submit. Becoming angry with God, they ran toward a worse pain, a pain absent of His presence. Instead of enduring the pain that the Lord allowed, they scattered left to right and far off course. Pain became their home.

The Lord clarified to me that in the coming days, we are going to have real conversations that bring forth real change. While in the womb of understanding, I saw the Deliverer calling to His Beloved. The Sun of Righteousness with fire in His eyes, and I heard His heart whisper with authority:

"Let's talk about pain."

The Lord showed me three different areas where people have separated themselves from Him. I am going to share about those later in this chapter. First, I must describe the friend of God. The friend of God will help reach those trapped in pain and bring them back to the way of true knowledge.

The Lord is rescuing His Beloved. There is a generation of people trapped in pain. We have a responsibility to help them find their way in Him. We must be a trusted leadership that encourages the broken into freedom.

The way is narrow, leading to life, and few will stay the course. Ultimately, there will be only a remnant that overcomes. They will overcome by the Lamb's blood and the word of their testimony. Divine revelation and a true encounter with God will always bring great change and activate life within us, bringing forth transformation. We will be blessed with greater authority and responsibility.

The Lord is prophesying to His Beloved: "It is time to receive the revelation and activate the transformation." This activation will be done through the friends of God.

The Lord has granted a remnant favor. To be anointed with this favor, we must be a friend worthy of God's trust. Through intimacy, we become the demonstration of Christ on the earth. A generation that will set the captives free. A chosen generation called out of darkness into His marvelous light. The friend of God is not interested in selfish gain. Complete companionship is his heart's desire. My husband, Paul Keith, interprets the friend of God like this:

> The friend of God! Such a distinction is clearly considered one of man's greatest honors. Even so, that opportunity is granted to those who abide in Christ, and His Word abides in them. The time has now arrived for the friends of Christ to begin to restore what has been stolen from the Church.

This favor is not granted to everyone. It is granted to those who are willing to be known by Him. Moses moved in mighty power and great terror. Sent by God, he performed signs and wonders in the sight of Israel, speaking to God face-to-face as a man speaks to his friend (see Exod. 33:11). Graced with the truest friend in God, Moses allowed himself to be known. It is written of Moses that the Lord knew him. I am certain that the intimacy Moses had with God will be a reality for trustworthy servants in this new era. They will move in His favor and turn many back from iniquity. Being a trustworthy friend is a necessary attribute to engage in revelatory encounters.

Many who are currently trapped in pain have a destiny to be united in friendship with God. He longs for this union. In some situations, He will operate through us to bring His Beloved back to the narrow way. At other times, the Lord Himself will call directly to their heart.

We see this return modeled in Matthew 26 and Luke 7. A beautiful woman came to Jesus just before His crucifixion. He reclined at the table as she approached Him with the alabaster jar. She poured perfume on His body to prepare Him for burial. This woman was considered by many in her day to be a sinner, a seemingly undeserving and foolish girl. In actuality, she's an overcomer. God called her out of a life of pain and gave her a revelation of who He is. Courageously she chose to receive her identity as one humble friend of God. Undeterred by the spirit of mockery, she went boldly, lavishing love upon the Lord. She was given a revelation to prepare the King. Understanding who He is set her free of a life of pain. Knowing Him brought forth her transformation—forgiven much and loved much.

The woman with the alabaster jar is symbolic of one of the three categories of people who will be set free. A trusted remnant will be given a battle plan to contend on behalf of the Bride of Christ. A trusted servant will express the mysterious wonders of Heaven. A trusted lover will invite the Lord to be intimately acquainted with all of her ways.

THE GIRL

"Let's talk about pain." These words compelled me to compassion. The Lord identifies the remnant making sure that none will suffer as a sinner. This identification is a perfect expression of His loving-kindness. *"Those also who suffer according to the will of God shall entrust their souls to a faithful Creator in doing what is right"* (1 Pet. 4:19).

As I sat with the Son in the womb of understanding, He revealed to me three categories of people He is identifying in this hour—the girl, the man, and the group.

The girl (representing a group just like her) had encountered pain along the narrow road. The pain had been too much for her to endure, so she froze in complete shock. She was unwilling to face pain; instead, she went into an alternate land. She began living in a fantasy designed through her wounds by some of the most complex parts of the human soul. The enemy is utilizing these illusions to keep her from her destiny.

I learned from Yeshua the depths of that pain. My compassion increased as He revealed the fear that lured her away. She must resist the devourer. The fear masquerades as debilitating pain. It is a convincing disguise that caused the girl to resist hope. There are two options, and only one will lead to deliverance:

1. Flee and hide in fear.
2. Be exposed in perfect love.

The Lord is beckoning her in love, drawing her back to the narrow way where the pain was first encountered. If she faces it with Him, she will suffer only for a little while; then, she will be confirmed by the God of all grace and continue on her journey. He will show Himself to her and heal her broken heart.

She was first created strong. She will return. The spirit of truth will guide her into all truth, and she will hope again with great discernment. Bold as Queen Esther. Full of love like Ruth. Brave of heart as Joan of Arc. With wisdom as solid as Harriet Tubman, Maria Woodworth-Etter, and Anna the intercessor. She will lead a movement led by Heaven's dreams.

> *Be of sober spirit, be on the alert. Your adversary, the devil, prowls around like a roaring lion, seeking someone to devour. But resist him, firm*

in your faith, knowing that the same experiences of suffering are being accomplished by your brethren who are in the world. After you have suffered for a little while, the God of all grace, who called you to His eternal glory in Christ, will Himself perfect, confirm, strengthen and establish you (1 Peter 5:8-10).

THE MAN

The journey endured within the realm of time is something quite amazing. The highs and lows of the hour change us, mold us, and too often define us. My past sorrows remind me how familiar all three categories are to me. I do not often recall the trials, but I have not forgotten where I came from or the moment the Deliverer called me out.

In honesty, take the opportunity to listen to His beckon and identify where you stand now. The narrow way calls to us and insists on a prompt response. For in denial and arrogance, people will perish. In the presence of His holiness, we are compelled to overcome.

Next, I saw a man with the heart of a boy. He was called before the foundation of the world to be a mature son, though he was unable to come to maturity because the conflict of his soul was too great. He, too, had been startled by the pain on this road. Instead of embracing the fullness of Christ, he embraced fear. From that point forward, everything he did was filtered through that fear. The fear became anger, and the anger became rage. That rage was thrown in the faces of everyone he claimed to love until love was a distant thought and no longer a reality for which he purposed.

It is not too late for him. The Lord is ever mindful and ever faithful. The man will come back to that painful memory that changed everything. Facing the pain, he will learn to deal with conflict and suffering in a healthy way. Courage will be his fuel. Submission will be his flame. Love will be his motivator.

Pain endured without the Son is not bearable; however, pain endured with Him will strengthen the soul and make firm the faith. It is one of the attributes of an overcomer. He will be immovable, receiving a kingdom that cannot be shaken. The overcomer will endure hardship as a good soldier offering to God an acceptable service with reverence and awe, for our God is a consuming fire (see Heb. 12:28-29).

> *If we died with Him, we will also live with Him; if we endure, we will also reign with Him; if we deny Him, He also will deny us; if we are faithless, He remains faithful, for He cannot deny Himself* (2 Timothy 2:11-13).

The Group

I have to take a moment to describe what was happening in the womb of understanding as the Lord revealed the third category. He continued to infuse rest and hope deep into my bones. The ribbon of pearl is a constant feed of life. This beautiful display of union affirmed that I am tethered to Him. I will never be separated nor abandoned. This revelation is a constant reality I embrace.

I recognized the ones I love in each of these different categories. I was no longer afraid for their destiny either. They are tethered to Him too. The Lord will call them and send His faithful friends to set them free.

The revelation was opened to me like a scroll. As the scroll opened, I grew in understanding. While the third group was revealed to me I could sense that my allotted time with the opened scroll was coming to an end. I paid close attention. I could feel how important it is to the Lord that I capture this insight. As the Lord shared the details, I listened intently. I heard the mercy call, the whisper in the wind of adversity; it is in the wind of the suffering found along the narrow way. I heard the whisper growing louder, calling them out of pain that was not intended for them.

I realized that we do not journey through life absent of pain. The narrow way that leads to life will include pain. There will also be a revelation of freedom in the suffering, despite the trial. Pain endured without the Son is unbearable. It is not what God has intended for us. Having encountered pain along the narrow way, this group reacted with hidden bursts of shame and hatred caused by the stings of fear. They refused to stand firm in the faith. Instead, they chose to suffer alone in self-pity with bouts of self-induced pain in the image of alcohol, drugs, eating disorders, self-mutilation, addiction, abusive relationships, and apathy. This group had gotten used to pain and made their home there.

The tragedy and loss in pain's home are unbearable because it is suffering endured without the Son. There is another home called love's home. The ways of love's home continue to compel me. Love's home drew me out of the pain of loneliness and set me in the ways of hope.

There is an urgent call, a mercy call that beckons the Beloved into the resting place found in love's home. Many of the Lord's people are currently scattered. Our honor is to gather them from the trenches, wide gate, and broken roads. We will gather and encourage them into perfect union. It is His design that they return to the narrow way.

In this new era we are going to talk about pain. We are going to learn how to deal with pain, and process through suffering. The girl, the man, and the group that left the narrow way were each searching for freedom from pain. Seeking to fill the emptiness that took up space in their soul, they ended up entangled in suffering that God was not present. The mercy call is a shout to deliver His children from deception's grip. We are gathering with Jesus—gathering the girl, the man, and the group. It is imperative that the Lord's people understand where they are suffering and whom they are suffering with. Who they are gathering and whom they are gathering with. They have a light to shine, a love to represent, and a destiny to fulfill.

THE VOID

This mystery's unveiling reminded me of my own deliverance from pain's void, which occurred many years ago. My compassion grew as I recalled the events from the morning that changed the course of my life.

I served the Lord for years, fasting, praying, teaching, operating in prophetic ministry, intercession, and service; however, I was unaware of the disruption brought on by unhealed trauma. I had done inner healing and was in constant pursuit of connection to the Lord; even so, the past wounds still had a lingering effect on my soul. What I am about to share is very personal. It is the end and the beginning. It is the moment of my resurrection.

It was early, and the sun was hidden behind the gray clouds of the fall morning here in Oregon. I had wrestled through night's terror and made it to sunrise. I could feel the day beckoning me. I did not realize that I was about to have an experience that would change me forever.

I was pulled in deep. I could feel the stretching of my flesh like the division of joints and marrow; it was the thoughts and intentions of my heart being judged. I saw the hands of the Lord come with defibrillators to jump-start my heart. I felt it blasting through my body and soul, a force of electricity that held me down. Unable to move, I was not sure if I was dying. I knew that my breath was getting weaker and my body more subdued.

Instantly I was pulled through a layer of skin, torturously stretched and brought into a massive empty space—the wretched void of emptiness.

I fell in. The most intense pain, sorrow, and loneliness filled this space. Aimless and distraught, desperate to escape this awful existence, I was falling, free falling into a never-ending pit. It felt as though I was not actually moving at all. I was stuck. I knew the Lord was the one allowing me to see the reality of such hell. Still, I could not feel His presence or guidance. I could not lean into His chest and find peace from the pain. He was not in this space. I hated the separation from Him and despised the existence of this place. I could not continue in this pain.

I will explain what happened next in a moment, but I first need to explain the separation. It has to be made clear, the agony of separation.

I knew it to be the worst kind of judgment—separation from the Father. When the ninth hour came, the Savior hung on the cross, darkness fell, and Jesus bore the sin of the world. The separation from the Father was described in such anguish as Jesus cried out with a loud voice saying, *"Eli, Eli, lama sabachthani?" That is, "My God, My God, why have You forsaken Me?"* (see Matt. 27:46). Spat on, beaten, mocked, and scourged, He hung, unrecognizable due to the incomprehensible abuse and pain He endured. The cry of forgiveness forever on His lips He endured this pain for you and me. The torment implemented by the enemies of the Lord was nothing compared to the pain of being separated from the Father at that moment that He bore all sin. He cried out again and yielded up His Spirit.

Separation from the Father will result in unbearable grief.

> *When the Lord Jesus will be revealed from heaven with His mighty angels in flaming fire, dealing out retribution to those who do not know God and to those who do not obey the gospel of our Lord Jesus. These will pay the penalty of eternal destruction, away from the presence of the Lord and from the glory of His power* (2 Thessalonians 1:7-9).

I understood that the sufferings found in the shallow of the void are all-consuming and have no end. The word *shallow* means "lacking in depth of knowledge, thought, or feeling." The wicked void is the enemy's attempt to come against true knowledge.

I hung there crying for help from the depths of the shallow. I was suspended in the atmosphere of a bottomless pit, exposed and absent of any protective boundaries. I understood later that I was in a realm of the soul. I tried with all my might to scream for help. I knew His Spirit and longed to feel His touch again. I was desperate for connection.

Suddenly, I was sucked through a layer of skin, almost like a membrane. In excruciating pain, I was squeezed back into the realm of time. From my experience in the spirit of knowledge (years later), I now understand that the skin signified a dimension change, including personal transformation.

The process of this deliverance was painful. Perhaps the void had become familiar to me, and letting go was burdensome. The Lord was bringing me into a place of healing and maturity that I had never walked before. The very void I was leaving was the void that took up space within me and kept me from the true knowledge of God.

First, He showed me the void. Then, He delivered me out of the void. Finally, He removed the void from me. In a moment, forever embedded in my memory, I left a dying land and entered Freedom's hands as He ripped desolation from my inner being. I heard the calming voice of the Father reach to me with mercy:

"I do not fill a void; I uproot a void."

I had been inside my own void, falling aimlessly. In that place, I was separated from my Creator. While pressing through that layer coming out of the void, I felt my body getting weaker and weaker. During this process, the state of my soul had been revealed. Sorrow had taken root long ago, and hope deferred caused sickness to spread in my heart. My heart was refusing to beat. The Lord, in all His mercy, was mindful of His story in me. His hands were steady as He jump-started my heart with defibrillators. He resurrected my life with hope. And just like that, my heart was no longer under cardiac arrest.

The Inner Man: Strong Enough for Love

Three days later, the Lord showed Himself to me again. I could hear the sounds of the past howling in the night, though the void no longer consumed me. I knew the Lord was mindful to help me find my way. Unexpectedly, I felt an incredible force strike me three times with steady and confident blows. Each strike proved painful, though different than the pain of letting go. This was a good pain, like the strengthening of new muscles. I was blasted by His hands of power three times in the core with a great demonstration of His might.

> *His splendor covers the heavens, and the earth is full of His praise. His radiance is like the sunlight; He has rays flashing from His hand, and there is the hiding of His power* (Habakkuk 3:3-4).

In compassion, He granted to me, according to the riches of His glory, to be strengthened with power through His Spirit in my inner man. He said:

"I have imparted strength in your inner man. You, being rooted and grounded in love, will experience lengths, widths, depths, and heights and know the love of Christ which surpasses knowledge that you may be filled up to all the fullness of God" (see Eph. 3:17-19).

Uprooting the void that kept me from the true knowledge of Him was an incredible display of grace. He did not stop there. Completing a good work in me, He proceeded to impart the greatest gift—strength in my inner man that I might explore the depths of love.

Those who overcome learn to deal with pain through holy surrender, resulting in abiding rest. Courage will be the motion in their march, expanding their capacity to love and shine. The more they deal with pain, the more fully they become light. This shine's brilliance is not a simple glimmer but confident rays of light that will captivate the masses.

The rays of light have force and purpose, ever expressing the spirit of might. Tethered to Him, the victorious ones will increase in knowledge, understanding, and all spiritual wisdom. This is the narrow way that leads to life.

> *That you may be filled with the knowledge of His will in all spiritual wisdom and understanding, so that you will walk in a manner worthy of the Lord, to please Him in all respects, bearing fruit in every good work and increasing in*

> *the knowledge of God; strengthened with all power, according to His glorious might, for the attaining of all steadfastness and patience; joyously giving thanks to the Father, who has qualified us to share in the inheritance of the saints in Light* (Colossians 1:9-12).

Chapter 5

Removing the Veil of Ignorance

It is with great expectation I await the revealing of the new day and the soaring ones who tell His story. The torchbearers will light up the sky with glory's glimmer and demonstrate the ways of an overcomer. The ones to carry off the victory are the peculiar ones, the last in line, and typically rejected. These victorious ones are created with an inspiration deep inside that will not let them quit, a fire in their belly motivating them to stand up and rise above.

Early one January morning, I was given insight that would clarify my expectations of the coming days and define the necessary qualifications of an overcomer. The Lord brought me into the realm of the Spirit. It felt more complex than a dream. I do not know that I have a name to identify it. I will call it a trance. My previous surroundings quickly faded into vanishing as I left the boundaries of time. I was unsure where I was headed or what I expected to see. I had been transported to this realm and could feel revelation inviting me.

I was navigating in a seemingly aimless manner along a busy city street; I could hear the buzzing of the cars and bustle of people scurrying about. I suddenly heard a noise that stood out above all the city's chaos.

I saw a man struggling to stand, nearly overcome with apathy and discouragement. I slowed my stroll down as I became more and more distracted by the burden he was dragging behind him on the concrete street. I could feel the intense impression of hopelessness erupting from his being. It was quite a sight—his head hanging over in despair, weakened legs, and tired eyes.

I felt compelled to restore him. His weary state tugged on my emotions and began to draw me in. I pulled back and steadied myself so that I would not be drawn into his weakness. I was pondering the situation when a woman approached. I briefly set aside the emotion I felt toward the man and shifted my attention toward the woman. I knew by the spirit that she had a message. I could still feel him and see him in my peripheral, but my focus shifted to the messenger. She looked fantastic, uninhibited, and brave. I was distracted by her presence in the greatest way. Immediately, I understood that she was one of the cloud of witnesses mentioned in Hebrews 11. She came to these busy streets of the city to encourage me along in my journey. She carried an important message of hope.

Leota's Story

I knew her in the land of the living before she passed. Her name is Lee. Though her life was filled with much struggle and little triumph, she had a remarkable ability to survive. She was born a great warrior.

The art of submission is an attribute of a true warrior. There is great honor in learning to let go of unnecessary opinions and yield to the will of the Father. It is laying down human authorship to be a part of a greater story. Some people fight against God's design using an irrevocable gift given to them by the Lord Himself. The irony of that always amazes me.

Human will is a marvelous phenomenon—the will and fight given by God and granted to a person so they would learn to lay it all down. Many people unknowingly work against God's plan using the very will He blessed them with. It took Lee a lifetime to learn the art of submission, though being a survivor was something she came into early and honestly. Lee had been born with the help of several midwives in a small house in Colorado. There were severe complications during Lee's delivery, beyond what the midwives were able to cure. Her father was filled with an overwhelming fight to contend on behalf of his daughter. He was not a spiritual man, though the Lord anointed him for the miraculous on this special day.

Stories like baby Lee's are seldom found in history books. It must be shared here to begin to understand the mysterious ways of the Lord. Complications during childbirth, likely caused by a blood disorder, took her mother's life and overwhelmed the lungs of baby Lee. At nine days old, the midwives figured little Lee for dead and denied her father's plea to take her with him. They informed him that she would not make it, claiming her fate was the same as her mother's. He could not accept their assessment and was unwilling to give up on his daughter's chance at life. Baby Lee had captivated his heart. Perhaps his unconditional love for her steered him toward the unexpected.

Maybe it was God compelling him to fight for His beloved daughter. Lee's father surprised hundreds of people over the course of many years with this valiant display of heroism. Those midwives did not understand, but they left him no other choice. Taking a shotgun into the midwifery house, baby Lee's daddy demanded that they give him his daughter. His wife had died during childbirth, and he was unwilling to believe his baby's life was over too. The midwives reluctantly handed over baby Lee. She was then driven by her father and grandmother (Little Grandma) to the children's hospital.

It was the middle of winter 1937 in Colorado. A snowstorm was blanketing the land. Traveling several hours across the Rocky Mountains, baby Lee's father longed to bring his precious girl to safety. Convinced that she was destined to live, he was compelled by a voice within him never to give up hope. He and his mother drove several hours on snow-saturated roads until they found their way to the children's hospital. Dropping droplets of milk in Lee's mouth in a courageous attempt to keep her alive, Little Grandma was baby Lee's first touch of comfort. The midwives, sticking to their original assessment of baby Lee, had contacted the children's hospital and let them know that there was a crazy man on his way with a shotgun, a little old lady, and a dead baby. Those midwives' assessment was wrong. Lee lived for 80 years.

She spent many years in grief over her mother's death and was rejected and resented by her mother's family. Raised by her father with Little Grandma's help, Lee began her search for family and connection at a very young age. She was married with her first child by the age of 14 years old. Not only had her mother died on her birthday, but Little Grandma did too. Lee's birthday was now an even more sorrowful memorial as she fought off fear and resentment with each passing year. Though the guilt she felt over Mother's death was often overwhelming, she never took the history of her miraculous survival and her father's heroic display of love lightly. He believed, against all odds, that she would live.

Lee endured 80 difficult years protecting a rich heritage ordained before the foundation of the world. She was in constant pursuit of a destiny she did not know how to reach and an inheritance she did not believe she was worthy of.

In 1957 in Los Angeles, California, Lee attended a Billy Graham crusade. She was compelled by that presence she had felt so many times throughout her life. The message of hope shared urged her to make a commitment to the Lord. She did not have anyone to teach her the ways of God but expressed her unique journey with His presence on many occasions. She felt His hand woven throughout her story, though she had little understanding of what it would mean to serve Him.

She had five kids by the age of nineteen, gave birth to seven kids total, and adopted two more. This strong woman was a completely flawed human, overwhelmed by the burden of raising so many children on her own, but she never gave up the fight. Lee worked hard. She knew how to survive, raising all her kids without the help of the government, family, or a supportive husband. Working day after day, there was no time spent crying over "wants," and she made this reality evident.

She was the only person these children had and devoted her days to see to it that they fulfilled their destinies, though she had little grid for what that even meant. For many years, fear had kept her bound, and tenderness was distant. God in all His compassion was bigger than fear's stings and stronger than her human will. He continuously drew her back to Him, time and time again.

She is a beautiful and tragic picture of an overcomer. Some overcomers are not identified by what they do for the duration of their lives but by the moment they lay their lives down. After many heart attacks, a stroke, and a couple of bouts with cancer, she realized her fight was fading. A drinker and a smoker, her lungs and body were failing. She was hanging on by pure grit. I spoke with her just months before she passed, standing in her apartment, surrounded by a handful of meaningful trinkets she had decided to hang on to. Each one was like a trophy to her, a display of her days.

Lee ran successful businesses early in her life, though she was not well educated, so her language was at times obscure. She spoke to me with an arrogance that was about to burst. "Amos, you know, I always been strong, I always be strong, I'm strong." I looked at her, filled with the compassion of Jesus, and responded, "You 'bout done?" She looked at me like I was crazy to speak so directly. Honestly, it may have taken all the courage of Heaven for me to speak so boldly to such a feisty woman.

As we visited together in her apartment, I was thankful to witness the miraculous. Lee learned the art of submission and received the greatest gift. Mindful of Lee, the Lord had graced this day and written it before the foundation of the world. That bubble of arrogance broke, and she began to weep. I felt compelled by the kindness of the Lord as He responded to her weeping through my words: "You have done a good job, and you have been strong for long enough. He desires to be your strength, your hero." She heard and received. She did a beautiful prayer and laid down her will, trading it for His design.

This is her moment of identification as an overcomer. This identification is more than merely justified, though justification is a beautiful destiny—to serve the Lord day and night. Confessing with her mouth in 1957 and believing in her heart could have been enough for justification. Still, there was plenty of uncertainty; her walk was contentious at times. Regardless, being simply justified was not God's design for her life. She was destined to be an overcomer, one who would carry in the victory.

> *He who overcomes, I will grant to him to sit down with Me on My throne, as I also overcame and sat down with My Father on His throne* (Revelation 3:21).

The commitment Lee made at Billy Graham's crusade and the many prayers she prayed with family were all part of her dance with God as He beckoned her to abide with Him in submission. Her destiny is to rule and reign with Him on His throne.

Overcomer

The word *overcomer* means "victorious one." Lee obediently stepped into her destiny of courage. Due to the overwhelming power of the yield, despite adversity, the spirit of this age was unable to vanquish the perfect design for Lee's life as an overcomer.

Judging by the first 79 years of her life, I am not sure that I would have expected her for an overcomer, seated in heavenly places. Though she had learned to fight, survive, and provide for her family, these were not the attributes that qualified her. It is submission that was her greatest act of valor. Many family members continually ministered the love of God to Lee and that day she finally chose to recognize her value—the same value her father saw that March morning, 1937. I am certain now that we would be surprised by whom the Lord calls overcomers and whom He does not. When Lee decided to receive the gift of life, lay down her story, and submit it all, she did more than ask the Lord for the forgiveness of sins; she completely yielded her will to the will of the Father.

> *But God, being rich in mercy, because of His great love with which He loved us, even when we were dead in our transgressions, made us alive together with Christ (by grace you have been saved), and raised us up with Him, and seated us with Him in the heavenly places in Christ Jesus, so that in the ages to come He might show the surpassing riches of His grace in kindness toward us in Christ Jesus. For by grace you have been saved through faith; and that not of yourselves, it is the gift of God; not as a result of works, so that no one may boast* (Ephesians 2:4-9).

> *He who has an ear, let him hear what the Spirit says to the churches. To him who overcomes, I will grant to eat of the tree of life which is in the Paradise of God* (Revelation 2:7).

Infusions of Hope

I had often pondered Lee's role as one of the cloud of witnesses and felt a great confirmation when I saw her in the spirit that January morning. After all the weariness she endured on earth, it was a sweet gift to see her with legs strong, face young, and eyes bursting with the joy of the Lord. The sounds of the busy city had faded in the distance. I was still longing to hear the message Lee was carrying in its entirety. My attention shifted quickly back to the burdened man on the street. I knew him as well. I knew him to be a leader of great valor. Why was he so burdened? What was he dragging behind him, and how would he combat against the spirit of slumber that attempted to take his destiny? Suddenly, I saw and understood as many others surrounded him, battling against the same enemy. Hope deferred had made their legs weak and hearts sick. They drug behind them old dreams—dreams formed in the heart of a man through opinion and selfish ambition. Tired and discouraged, these leaders would surely lose their way if the Lord did not intervene.

I watched as the Lord sent messengers to strengthen the leaders, infusing His Beloved with righteous ambition, desire, and hope. The hope was inspired in the abiding, inspired in the union. No longer weary, given the desire to go another lifetime, these valiant forerunners were quickly being equipped with 2 Corinthians 5:6-9:

> *Therefore, being always of good courage, and knowing that while we are at home in the body we are absent from the Lord—for we walk by faith, not by sight—we are of good courage, I say, and prefer rather to be absent from the body and to be at home with the Lord. Therefore we also have as our ambition, whether at home or absent, to be pleasing to Him.*

I watched His beloved leaders receive the antidote, infusions deep into their bones. The heavy burden of unfulfilled dreams was left there on that city street. Infusions of hope encouraged them to dream again and strengthened their legs to run. With tongues as the pen of a ready writer, grace upon their lips, arms prepared to build and wings to soar above the sorrows of the land, they are a picture of the submitted ones, leaving behind the old ways and yielding to perfect design. They were given more than endurance; they were given desire.

This January morning, it felt as though I truly walked those city streets. Far beyond simple dreaming, it was a journey in the unseen realm. I was thankful to celebrate with these leaders as the Lord corralled us all with His goodness. I watched each leader closely for a moment as their eyes began to celebrate the ways of His Kingdom again. The strength of their constitution seemed to return. Hope saturated the atmosphere, our paths dripped with the abundance of Heaven. It was a sight to see the vibrations of rejoicing fill those city streets.

The Second Show

Lee was still behind me; I heard her hollering for my attention. I stopped, focused intently on her as she firmly delivered a message. The words penetrated through my soul and took root deep in my heart. It was for and about the remnant. She spoke directly and sternly. "The second show will soon begin. It is not a broad way! It will display the mature. The mature will have access to greater authority than ever before. Authority purposed for abiding and drawing the Beloved into a place of perfect union."

I was given a deeper understanding of Scriptures, interpretation, and revelation after my experience in the realm of the spirit of knowledge. It was one of the gifts acquired in that realm. The Word of the Lord and the messages from His messengers come with greater clarity than ever before. The spirit of knowledge heightens discernment. Lies are more blatantly pronounced and obviously exposed. As well, revelation from God appeared to me with a more precise pitch, color, and fragrance. I knew the message from Lee carried a great weight from Heaven as it began to expound the following Scripture:

> *Enter through the narrow gate; for the gate is wide and the way is broad that leads to destruction, and there are many who enter through it. For the gate is small and the way is narrow that leads to life, and there are few who find it* (Matthew 7:14).

It will not be a "broad" way. The road that leads to life is narrow, and the remnant will not pierce those boundaries. They will yield themselves in the path of justice. There is an expression of His Spirit coming through those who will journey in the narrow way. It will be a demonstration of Kingdom authority and will draw a people into beautiful union. The second show will soon begin, a presentation grander than the first.

> *"The latter glory of this house will be greater than the former," says the Lord of Hosts, "and in this place I will give peace"* (Haggai 2:9).

The Preparation

Lee was no longer with us, though I had hoped to draw from the wisdom she carried. The leaders were still gathered behind me, rejoicing as the Lord continued to encounter and heal them. The injections of hope and excitement they received were, in part, an equipping. I perceived this equipping was for something massive—a final demonstration of leadership, maturity, and glory.

That they would live in the Spirit according to the will of God for the culmination of all things is near (see 1 Pet. 4:7).

Suddenly, I was in a beautiful auditorium. Few seats were taken, and the curtains were drawn. I could tell by the regal design of the viewing area that a glorious show was about to take place. A royal priesthood—mature sons of God, a people for God's own possession—would take the stage, proclaiming and demonstrating the excellencies of Him who has called us out of darkness and into His marvelous light (see 1 Pet. 2:9).

I remembered the words Lee spoke: "The second show will soon begin! It is not a broad way! It will display the mature!" I felt it burning in my bones—this was going to be an epic show! The culmination of all things is near, and mature sons of God will soon tell the greatest story. A demonstration of submission, union, and reverential awe. The story of the overcomers who suffered according to God's will and entrusted their souls to a faithful Creator (see 1 Pet. 4:19).

There were now new words traveling toward me, words calling from the distance. The words were not too far away, though they have not arrived yet either. I heard them clearly, and I saw them travel through time, bouncing off the walls of what looked like sound waves until they reached me. I could feel the urgency to pull the words in. I knew these words would be relevant one day:

"It is showtime! It is time for teamwork, expression, and union!"

I could see and feel the pitter-patter of feet behind the curtains. I connected the equipping that those leaders received on the city streets to the preparation happening backstage. The Lord's Beloved was being made ready. In a moment, I understood the importance of being made ready. Preparation is a beautiful part of the show. These were not your average backstage antics. No makeup. No costumes. No masks, for she carries no shame. No lines to rehearse, for the Word has been branded upon her heart. Behind the curtain was perfect hiddenness with Christ, His Beloved being lavished with truth.

I could hear the melody of love in the secret place—a deluge of grand gestures. Showtime is drawing near, and I feel the countdown pulling me to its reveal. Consumed by truth, the Beloved will express her great value and character while demonstrating the power of the yield. I am moved by the reality that our identity in Christ shapes the new era; it is the light of the second show. In holiness and reverence, He will form the new day.

In integrity, the shining ones will tell the story of the brightest days. Clothed in regal attire, completely apprehended by His beauty, the spirit of wisdom will release the words of Heaven in one final display, the beautiful display of union and reverential awe.

Soulish ambition, toil, and self-promotion weakened the leaders before. We will not fall into that trap again. The second show will not be a one-man show nor performed by arrogant, boastful, treacherous lovers of pleasure. Quite the contrary—submission, unity, and the reverential fear of the Lord will fuel their demonstration.

The overcomers are a unified force who will refuse to bow to religious or political agendas for selfish gain. In deep reverence for God, they will join the four living creatures and the 24 elders, never ceasing to give glory and honor and thanks to Him who sits on the throne, never ceasing to declare His splendor.

The Veil of Ignorance

I was both behind the curtains preparing to tell His story and observing the stage from the viewing area. On the outside of the curtains the word *ignorance* was written. I observed from a bird's-eye view as the curtain was being removed from every direction. The veil of ignorance was removed. Paul shared about this ignorance to the men of Athens:

> *I observe that you are very religious in all respects. For while I was passing through and examining the objects of your worship, I also found an altar with this inscription, "TO AN UNKNOWN GOD." Therefore what you worship in ignorance, this I proclaim to you. The God who made the world and all things in it, since He is Lord of heaven and earth, does not dwell in temples made with hands; nor is He served by human hands, as though He needed anything, since He Himself gives to all people*

> *life and breath and all things; and He made from one man every nation of mankind to live on all the face of the earth, having determined their appointed times and the boundaries of their habitation, that they would seek God... "For we also are His children." Being then the children of God, we ought not to think that the Divine Nature is like gold or silver or stone, an image formed by the art and thought of man. Therefore having overlooked the times of ignorance, God is now declaring to men that all people everywhere should repent, because He has fixed a day in which He will judge the world in righteousness through a Man whom He has appointed, having furnished proof to all men by raising Him from the dead* (Acts 17:22-31).

In the previous show, ignorance had been a veil. A generation of people were darkened in their understanding because of the ignorance that was in them and the hardness of their heart (see Eph. 4:18). In reverence and repentance, those curtains will be removed. Once the veil is removed, this new day will reveal maturity. It is a display of splendor, awe, and reverence through those who have been enlightened and have tasted the heavenly gift (see Heb. 6:4). This new show is the new day.

The reverential fear of the Lord will remove the veil of ignorance and give a chosen generation access to the mysteries of His heart, demonstrating a full assurance of hope until the end. They will be convinced of that which accompanies salvation, including authority in the realm of the Spirit—authority purposed for abiding and drawing the Beloved into a place of perfect union.

The reverent will light the atmosphere with the wisdom of God and push back a spirit of darkness currently deceiving a generation. This authority will bring in the greatest harvest the world has ever seen. The Lord will have His harvest. Some of this harvest are identified as "overcomers" who will rule and reign with Him on His throne. A larger portion will know salvation but will not learn to yield. While they will spend eternity glorifying the Lord, serving Him day and night, they will not rule with Him on His throne. Still, the Lord's remnant will shine and the world will see it. The second show will be a demonstration of His power to bring many to righteousness. Here, they will rejoice in the salvation of the Lord.

> *The people who were sitting in darkness saw a great Light, and those who were sitting in the land and shadow of death, upon them a Light dawned* (Matthew 4:16).

CHAPTER 6

THE STORES OF HEAVEN

Before the end of the age, all that has been sealed up will be revealed. The Lord will proclaim to His remnant new things from this time, even hidden things which we have not known. By virtue of the seven lamps of fire, this generation will be equipped to access that which has been concealed in the treasury rooms until the appointed time. There is an allotted time when the remnant will be approved to express the creations granted to them and accessed from the depths of these storehouses—treasures that will be the stability of their times, a wealth of salvation, wisdom, and knowledge. In these days He is exalted and will favor Zion, filling her with justice and righteousness.

The Lord will supply all our needs according to His riches in glory in Christ Jesus. Our provider and the One who sees ahead continues to gift His people with provisions necessary for the season. He fills and equips His

Beloved with vats filled to overflowing. He gives to us from the plentitude of the earth, the abundance of the fruit of His creation.

The treasury rooms reach far beyond that which is carried in the vessels of the land; they are hidden in the stores of Heaven and are not for simple provision. What is found in the treasure rooms will mobilize a generation. Even as He sends ministering spirits to render service for the sake of those who will inherit salvation (see Heb. 1:14), the treasuries are not to glorify that which will perish, but are gifts, eternal attributes that will express His love to a generation.

> *Do not store up for yourselves treasures on earth, where moth and rust destroy, and where thieves break in and steal. But store up for yourselves treasures in heaven, where neither moth nor rust destroys, and where thieves do not break in or steal. For where your treasure is, there your heart will be also* (Matthew 6:19-21).

He declared the former things long ago, and they went forth from His mouth. Suddenly He acted, and they came to pass. Surely His hand founded the earth, and His right hand spread out the heavens. He called to them, and they stood together (see Isa. 48:13). The stars and the moon and all flowers and shrubs of the land stand for their allotted time, displaying His splendor. But they will wear out like a garment, changing; however, the Lord who is exalted, His throne remains forever!

The storehouses hold the deep where awe inspires. They hold the perfect supply of riches glorified in the Christ and drawn up in the heart of the Father. These rooms' gifts are from the attributes of God—His wind (His Spirit), goodness, manifold wisdom, discernment, awe and reverence, vengeance, and compassion.

The treasury rooms hold the mysteries of change ushered in by the wind. The hallowed Name responds from the depths with a manifestation of His nature, causing the breakers and waves of His Spirit to wash over us even as the deep calls to deep.

> *When He utters His voice, there is a tumult of waters in the heavens, and He causes the clouds to ascend from the end of the earth; He makes lightning for the rain, and brings out the wind from His storehouses* (Jeremiah 10:13).

The release of His breath set up creation and established the earth's solid foundation. It is life, courage, and the certainty that He is the One true living God.

The wind stored up in the treasuries is to be released upon the fullness of time in order to execute proper order in the Kingdom of God. In our pursuit of personal fulfillment, it is imperative to restrain from moving ahead of our allotted time. We must wait for the favorable wind of the Spirit.

The Winds and the Deeps

In a strategic dream it was revealed to me the necessary attributes of a leader and the cruciality of timing when taking off into their calling. I was shown the heart of one well-known, controversial yet influential leader named William Branham—a man of integrity, a forerunner of forerunners, with a heart purposed for the things of the Kingdom.

Branham grew up without any knowledge of God, the Bible, or prayer. He was born into massive poverty and endured extreme social rejection and ridicule. The son of a womanizing, perverse alcoholic with a reputation for impropriety, Branham wrestled through the early years, even overcoming death. As a boy, he had limited academic education and never learned the ways of church or healthy lifestyle. Yet amidst all of the lack, struggle, and chaos, still the Lord continued to pursue and teach him. Branham learned the ways of God through encounter. Miraculous experiences taught him the character and essence of God. He understood being experientially known. These experiences included directional encounters that led to hundreds of thousands of healings and salvations.

The Lord's hands sovereignly guided Branham through his life teaching the secrets of the Kingdom. On the morning of April 6, 1909, in a little mountain cabin with no rugs or wood on the floor, he was born. As the afternoon rolled in, they recognized a mysterious light had whirled into the room and hovered over the bed where he was lying. This was the beginning of a lifelong journey with the supernatural. God continued from this day forward to highlight Branham, direct him, and call to him from the winds and the deeps.

His first encounter would set the stage for a life of submission. When he was just seven years old, he was bringing water to his father's moonshine still. A whirlwind came in the top of a tree, and a voice spoke out of it, saying, "Do not ever smoke or drink or defile your body in any way, for there will be a work for you to do when you get older."

In the years that followed this instruction, the Lord encountered William Branham time and time again.

May 1946 he had returned home from his job as a game warden. He exited his truck and started walking toward the house when suddenly a supernatural wind whirled in the tree next to him and knocked him down to the ground. This supernatural event motivated him to relentlessly pursue the Lord for answers. He told his wife of all the past experiences of the wind rushing above him in the trees. He made the decision to go to his secret cabin to pray and find out what these supernatural occurrences were. He intended to wait it out with God until he had a true understanding. At 3:00 a.m. that morning, the angel of the Lord appeared before him, commissioning him into one of the greatest healing ministries of all time.

Signs, wonders, healings, and miracles followed his ministry as his fame spread rapidly. Crowds were drawn to the supernatural stories and divine healings that would take place at his meetings. Clearly, the Lord's favor was upon him. He was not driven by selfish ambition nor motivated by personal agenda; he was compelled by a design much grander than human design. Through trial and conflict he learned the art of submission. Truly a yielded vessel with no desire to go beyond the boundaries of God, William Branham's submission to divine design is a model of what is to come.

I saw in a dream the three qualities that Branham possessed, which will also be revealed through faithful servants in the coming days. These attributes will demonstrate true integrity and train the remnant in the ways of submission. Those three qualities are:

1. The ability to release what is not their responsibility
2. The ability to release their will
3. The ability to release their spirit

The ability to release our agenda and submit to God's timeline will be crucial in the coming days. There is freedom in the boundaries of the Lord. Freedom's wind is a beautiful rush, powerful momentum that can quickly launch a person or a ministry. On the contrary, those who attempt to come forth out of their appointed time will miss their divine call resulting in discipline or even destruction.

After I was given the three qualities of William Branham, I was quickly brought to a runway. Instantly I knew this was a cautionary message, a warning for the leaders of today. On a runway sat several planes preparing for takeoff. There was a proper order and rank for their flight. There were few, faithful and true, who were patiently waiting for their release.

I cringed as I witnessed many young, well-meaning "pilots" attempting to rush their takeoff. They found it to be no conflict in their soul to bump others out of the way even attempting to fly in the favor of another. They were destined to one day lead a flight but not before their time. Ignoring the instruction and wisdom of the seasoned pilots, human ambition drove them. Attempting to take off quickly, outside of their allotted time, resulted in destruction. As they took off, it was as though they hit a brick wall, knocking them down violently.

Qualified pilots understand restraint and wait patiently on the runway. They carry the ability to release what is not theirs, submit their opinions, and yield up their spirit. This gives them access to the deeps of the storehouses where the wind is favorable. They will know the Lord's breath and wait in reverential fear for His command.

> *He lays up the deep in storehouses. Let all the earth fear the Lord; let all the inhabitants of the world stand in awe of Him. For He spoke, and it was done; He commanded, and it stood fast* (Psalm 33:7-9).

SOUND WISDOM

His glory will be vastly demonstrated through a generation that reveres Him. He will gift the earth with the miraculous again, and the remnant will shine like the firmament in her allotted hour. Graced with manifold wisdom and discernment, she will be equipped for both battle and dance. Though it has been spoken and described in song and rhyme, in picture and parable, still there are created miracles that will be a surprise for His Bride. Lavished with splendor and beauty, He will reveal to her things eye has not seen and ear has not heard, nor have they entered into the heart of man. These storehouses hold that which God has prepared for those who love Him (see 1 Cor. 2:9)—a blessing of eternal magnitude gifted to those who revere Him and stand in awe of His name. The reverent generation will unseal these mysteries, for the presence of God both inspires and is inspired by awe. The fear of the Lord is His treasure.

In this hour He will bring to light that which for ages has been hidden in God who created all things, so that the manifold wisdom of God might now be made known. For He stored up sound wisdom for the upright—a shield for her so that she will walk in integrity even in the darkest hour. In this hour there will be nothing hidden from its heat. Through grace He will strengthen them with power through His Spirit in the inner man so that Christ will dwell in their hearts through faith. For in joy, He breathed the existence of the earth and shared with humanity the array of artwork making up this land and the heavens that declare His glory. In love, He created His Beloved beautifully in His image and has marked each member with a great variety of colors, having created all of this in order to display and make known His manifold wisdom.

Christ Jesus—who became wisdom from God, righteousness, sanctification, and redemption—will cause the masses to glory in His name. He will demonstrate the spirit of wisdom and pour it out through a chosen generation, confounding the wise of this world. For He has chosen the foolish to put to shame the wise and the weak to put to shame that which is mighty in the land for this purpose: *"That no flesh should glory in His presence"* (1 Cor. 1:29 NKJV). When the secrets of the self-righteous are revealed and exposed, the godless will be driven away. They will be unable to look at the face of holiness; Jehovah Tsidkenu (the Lord Our Righteousness) will cause His light to radiate from the faces of the elect in all wisdom with understanding.

For those who in selfish ambition have removed their hearts from Him and have brought extreme disorder to the land, He will again deal marvelously with them, and the wisdom of their wise men will perish, and the discernment of their discerning men will be concealed. For the wisdom of this world is earthly, natural, and demonic (see James 3:15). However, there is a peculiar people, unbeknownst to the wise of this world, that will stand in awe of the God of Israel, light up the land, and manifest the wisdom of Heaven that is pure, peaceable, and unwavering.

GOODNESS

How great is God's goodness, which He has stored up for those who fear Him, which He has prepared for those who trust in Him. For the coming years will be crowned with His goodness and our paths will drip with abundance (see Ps. 65:11). The coming days are not a fantasy but a reality we are destined to. Those who believe and obey will see the goodness of the Lord in the land of the living. His goodness will be poured out to and through His elite.

The goodness of the Lord will include the wealth of nations. There will be a distribution of financial provision to a community established and surrounded in His goodness. Then you shall see and become radiant; the radiance of this light will reach a generation. And your heart shall swell with joy because the abundance of the sea shall be turned to you, and the wealth of the Gentiles shall come to you (see Isa. 60:5).

There will be a manifestation of supernatural wealth transfer, an abundance that has been stored up in the depths (sea), and as the deep calls unto deep, the depths will respond with favor. It is not for the sake of wealth that we will access the storehouses. In humble desire a remnant will access His mysteries for concern of personal character growth, power evangelism, and connection to the Father; however, His goodness is directly connected to His abundance. From the fruit of His Spirit, of the overflow of His goodness, will come provisional miracles that will inspire awe and glorify His glorious house.

Drawing from the treasure room of His goodness, we will be given access to the mysteries of divine health, renewal, and restoration. Satisfying the years with good things, He will renew our youth like the eagle, even as He made these ways known to Moses (see Ps. 103:5-7). Moses was 120 years old when he died; his eye was not dim nor his vigor abated (see Deut. 34:7). The Lord took him; the Lord buried him. However, his body was still strong. Abraham and Sarah were blessed with the goodness of the Lord. She gave birth to Isaac when she was advanced in age, though likely young in appearance and physicality. These heroes of the faith were experientially known by His goodness.

Jesus of Nazareth, who is fully God and walked the earth in human form, *"went about doing good and healing all who were oppressed by the devil"* (Acts 10:38). Emotional and spiritual freedom is a result of His goodness. In these days His goodness will be expressed in lavish affection healing many in the area of touch. I saw that there had been boundary violations and extreme physical abuse that have caused many of the Lord's Beloved to retreat, denying healthy touch for fear of pain again. I saw the Lord's angel reach His hand into the storehouse of Heaven and pull a fireball of goodness, hurling it on to the earth. This goodness will not only heal the brokenhearted in the area of touch but will bring forth an abundance of joyful memories in a short amount of time. This is part of the process to rewire thinking and shift the Beloved into creative exploration.

Creativity sharpens the mind and releases negative emotions. Ingenuity and creativity are important to the Lord and directly connected to His goodness. For in the beginning God created the heavens and the earth. God said, *"Let there be light,"* and there was light. He called forth light and saw that it was good. Even when the Lord let the dry land appear, called it earth, then gathered together the waters, He saw that it was good. He brought forth the grass, the seeds, the fruit. He created all living creatures and saw that it was good (see Gen. 1). The Lord still continues to create new things to inspire awe and cause His creation to glorify His name (see Isa. 43).

The sweetness of His goodness reaches all of our senses; it is our great pleasure to taste and see. There will be no lack or need, but in reverence there will be complete fulfillment. Restored wealth, strengthened bodies, renewed minds, healed emotions, time miracles, and ingenuity are just a few expressions of His goodness accessed in the storehouses of Heaven. The fear of the Lord is the sweetest treasure giving access to all that is good.

> *The angel of the Lord encamps around those who fear Him, and rescues them. O taste and see that the Lord is good; how blessed is the man who takes refuge in Him! ...For those who fear Him there is no want* (Psalm 34:7-9).

VENGEANCE AND COMPASSION

> *"Is it not laid up in store with Me, sealed up in My treasuries? Vengeance is Mine, and retribution, in due time their foot will slip; for the day of their calamity is near, and the impending things are hastening upon them." For the Lord will vindicate His people, and will have compassion on His servants* (Deuteronomy 32:34-36).

Keep your eyes open and your hearts awake; He will manifest His anger for compassion's sake! Keep your eyes open, for the passions of God will be manifest on the earth. Great anger will rage forth like a tumult of water, expressed for compassion's sake. Woe to him who builds a city on innocent blood. Let the remnant find refuge while indignation runs its course, for He will deal with their dealings.

Vengeance is coming to judge a system that was not ordained by God. This corrupted system is the representation of a people without reverence.

Recompense is when the Lord will judge the hearts of men, whether humble and contrite or wicked and ever scheming. The Lord will judge accordingly, for He is avenger in all these things. He will expose the wicked and reveal the reverent.

For the remnant will stand in reverential fear of Him, and from them He will not turn away. Since we have confidence to enter the Most Holy Place by the blood of Jesus and the revelation of the Name, and since we have a great priest over the house of God, let us draw near to God with a sincere heart and with the full assurance that faith brings, having our hearts sprinkled to cleanse us from a guilty conscience and having our bodies washed with pure water. Let us hold on to hope, for He is faithful.

> *If we deliberately keep on sinning after we have received the knowledge of the truth, no sacrifice for sins is left, but only a fearful expectation of judgment and of raging fire that will consume the enemies of God. Anyone who rejected the law of Moses died without mercy on the testimony of*

> *two or three witnesses. How much more severely do you think someone deserves to be punished who has trampled the Son of God underfoot, who has treated as an unholy thing the blood of the covenant that sanctified them, and who has insulted the Spirit of grace? For we know him who said, "It is mine to avenge; I will repay," and again, "The Lord will judge his people." It is a dreadful thing to fall into the hands of the living God* (Hebrews 10:26-31 NIV).

Regretfully, many still insult the Spirit of grace by wearing the stains of shame as a cloak either by never coming to the true knowledge of forgiveness or by continuing to live a sinful life. The deception displayed in the hyper grace movement, where reverence appears irrelevant, is equally appalling. It is for compassion's sake that we have been given this access to the Father, who is deity incomprehensible and worthy of full honor and respect. There is no balance between shame and hyper grace, for both are of utter disrespect of the Son and the price paid for our purity. A true revelation of the power of the blood and fullness of the Name will cause His people to appropriately and confidently display grace.

Knowing the fear of the Lord, we persuade men having a sound mind because love controls us. He has committed to us the word and ministry of reconciliation, which is of utmost importance to the Lord. It is for compassion's sake He bore my shame. God was in Christ reconciling the world to Himself, not counting their trespasses against them. Positively the most beautiful exchange, His righteousness for our guilt. And He has destined and established in us the divine message of this great exchange—the message of the restoration of favor. In reverence we will minister the restoration of favor (reconciliation) to His people in the hope that they receive the truth and live in connection to God. There is nothing more painful than separation from the Father. Jesus Himself offered up prayers with many tears; He shrank in horror at the thought of separation from the Father (see Heb. 5:7 AMPC). It is for the sake of adoption that He has called us into connection with Him. He is the motivation for our destiny and the reason we are overcomers. It is with this understanding that we are expectant as we gather the Beloved and encourage her into the arms of a loving Father. Jesus said:

> *He who is not with Me is against Me; and he who does not gather with Me scatters* (Matthew 12:30).

Those who gather will be recognizable. Knowing the fear of the Lord, they will persuade men and be carriers of the message of the great exchange. They will carry the true message of grace and the ministry of reconciliation. Anything contrary to the ministry of reconciliation is as enmity to God. It is blasphemy and a complete displeasure to the Lord.

The word *blasphemy* in the Greek means "showing contempt or lack of reverence for God, gross irreverence." This would include denying prophetic power, healing power, and resurrection power. Those irreverently busying about, embracing a lie, teaching a lie, and denying the fullness of the power in the Name of Jesus will draw the vengeance and judgment of the Lord. For this is the rejection of grace.

The word *blasphemy* in Hebrew means "to pierce, to pierce with holes, curse, puncture." God allowed blasphemy on His body for the sake of reconciliation. He suffered shame, guilt, and death on our behalf for the Beloved's eternal connection to the Father. Blasphemy pierced through His hands and speared His side; persecution lashed upon His back. For in all the days of His flesh, He prayed to the One who was always able to save Him from death. Because of His reverence, His prayers were heard (see Heb. 5:7). But in the very moment when the Son bore hell, sin, and all irreverence, there was a separation from the Father. Though the Son cried in agony to see the bright presence of God, instead He was judged for the blasphemy (irreverence) and sin of the world with death and momentary separation from the Father.

> *About the ninth hour* [Yeshua] *cried out with a loud voice, saying, "Eli, Eli, lama sabachthani?"*

> *that is, "My God, My God, why have You forsaken Me?"* (Matthew 27:46)

There was temporary separation between Him and the Father. He bore all sin and hell and endured the pain of separation.

> *And Jesus cried out again with a loud voice, and yielded up His spirit. And behold, the veil of the temple was torn in two from top to bottom; and the earth shook and the rocks were split* (Matthew 27:50-51).

Blasphemy is to reject the Holy Spirit. This is done by believers all the time, by those who claim to have accepted the blood for remission of their sins. Reverential submission is the message of the Father's heart—an expression of honor and gratitude for the price paid on the cross. This is a message we must become in order to be truly pleasing to the Lord, in addition to gathering His people and teaching them the true ways of grace. We now preach a message of being reconciled; there is not a place allowed to blaspheme His Spirit.

> *Therefore I say to you, any sin and blasphemy shall be forgiven people, but blasphemy against the Spirit shall not be forgiven. Whoever speaks a word against the Son of Man, it shall be forgiven him; but whoever speaks against the*

> *Holy Spirit, it shall not be forgiven him, either in this age or in the age to come* (Matthew 12:31).

Speaking a word against the Holy Spirit will affect their position in this age and the age being prepared for us. The word translated as *age* here is the word *aión*. Mark describes his account and uses the Greek word *aiónios,* which is a variation of the word, implying a cycle of time, especially present age as contrasted with the future age. Age-long is therefore practically eternal but not unending.

The phrase "will not be forgiven" in this verse comes from a Greek word *aphieme,* which means "will abandon, divorce, send away." The judgment here is separation from the Father for this age and the one being prepared. What a wretched existence, separation from the Father. The overcomers, who have lived a yielded life, will be qualified to participate in the age to come and rewarded based on their deeds in the body, according to what they have done either good or bad (see 2 Cor. 5:10).

Ultimately, the Lord is the avenger in all things wicked and vile. He will manifest vengeance beyond simple discipline. It will be for the sake of compassion for those who revere Him and possess their own vessel in sanctification and honor. There is a blatant disregard of holiness that simply will not be acceptable. We are gathering those destined to serve Him and teaching them the ways of grace. A higher standard is set for the Bride of Christ. A line of demarcation that cannot be penetrated.

In accessing the treasures of vengeance and compassion, laid up in the storehouses, we are accessing the full gift of grace *and* judgment. Compassion is the nature of His heart to heal and reconcile Himself to us. Anything that stands in the way will be dealt with severely. The unity of the faith and the true knowledge of God are the prophetic promise for the Bride—a promise that continues to motivate us in the ways of grace. The true remnant of God's people have an ever-increasing longing for connection and an utter disdain for blasphemy. They will hate the rampant wickedness with in the Church. It is soon that we will see a manifestation of perfect recompense—His justice for all to see.

The Lord will judge these systems. There is a company of the reverent that will continue to call His people out of idolatry and gather the Beloved into union. There is a chosen generation that longs to see the brightness of His face and is willing to yield to the designs of grace. They will stand for righteousness and will magnify the Name above all names.

CHAPTER 7

EXPANSIONS OF AUTHORITY, TIME, AND SPACE

"As the early church was miraculously birthed with accelerated growth, time miracles, signs and wonders, and an extraordinary demonstration of the spirit so shall it be at the end of the age when that same kind of miracles are performed once again in amplified ways."

—PAUL KEITH DAVIS

There is coming an Enoch community that will demonstrate the reality of time—not on a timeline but rather as an ever-expanding opportunity, also known as authority, given to the overcomers and found in abiding. The Lord, having made from one man every nation of mankind to live in all the face of the earth, determined their appointed times and the boundaries of their habitation (see Acts 17:26).

This intelligently designed cooperation enables the communication of all living creatures on the earth. Functioning in proper accord, they execute time and even divine appointments as designed and appropriated by the Lord. The order that we call "appointed time" is an allotment of authority prescribed.

For the Lord has prepared the lights of the firmament spreading out the heavens. The stars ornament the sky, hang in their appointed places on the orders of the Holy One. At His command they do not rest. Whatever the Lord commands will be done at the appointed time. He gives the sun authority to shine and appointed the moon for its seasons.

The sun is a dynamic instrument that brings the heat at midday and fresh hope in the morning, existing as a constant source of life with authority to release light and power. Still, this fire that radiates in the heavenlies functions in order at its proper time and does not transgress its law or move beyond the boundaries of its habitation. The Lord Most High sets those boundaries on the earth. He does whatever He pleases—in Heaven and in earth, in the seas and in the deep places (Ps. 135:6).

Every part of creation moves in an order as directed by the Most High, moving in patterns, even as the weather. *"He disperses the cloud of His lightning. It changes direction, turning around by His guidance, that it may do whatever He commands it on the face of the inhabited earth"* (Job 37:11-12).

Everything in creation is given authority or access for a certain function. The Enoch community will operate in Heaven's authority, having been given the keys to the Kingdom of Heaven. These mature sons will be given more access and more space to tell His story. They will do in a short amount of time what once took a really long time to do. This community will understand that their habitation's expanding boundaries are not just geographical locations but an expansion of authority in the Spirit. They will be given more room to demonstrate His wisdom, inspiring awe, and reverence.

The Enoch community understands the communication of the eternal realm. They have access to travel in and out of time as the Lord allows. They look not at things seen, but at the things which are not seen; for the things seen are temporal, but the things which are not seen are eternal (see 2 Cor. 4:18).

They will be given authority to go beyond the boundaries of time. Enoch was not found because God took him up. In continued pursuit of true knowledge, the Enoch community will walk with God and be granted authority to defy typical time boundaries. They will have jurisdiction over space (which we call time) to extend and shorten at their word by His command.

Paul Keith describes an example of this in an excerpt he wrote entitled "The Day the Lord Listened to the Voice of a Man":

> One of the most amazing stories in all of scripture is found in Joshua 10:12-14. The day the sun stood still and the moon stopped. Israel was in the midst of a heated battle with the Amorites. Joshua needed more time for the battle to be complete. So he prayed this amazing prayer: "O sun, stand still at Gibeon, and O moon in the valley of Aijalon."
>
> And the sun stood still and the moon stopped until Israel defeated their enemies. We are told there has been no day like it before or after. What truly transpired? Almighty God the Creator of the universe overshadowed the battlefield with a timeless dimension that caused the sun to stand in its place and the moon to remain until the words of Joshua were completed.
>
> The Lord is the God of time. I saw the Lord in an open vision holding time like a ruler. I heard him say, "This is time for time is measured." From His eternal posture He sees all of time simultaneously. The Lord lives in the eternal realm that is timeless. In some fashion known only to God, that timeless realm overshadowed

> the battlefield that day and allowed Israel to do the impossible.
>
> I believe in these last days the Lord will once again miraculously heed the voice of anointed vessels who speak on His behalf. It will be the ministry of the "spoken word." It says in Mark 11 if we say to this mountain, "Be removed and cast into the sea," it will obey. There is coming a day that a body of people will be in such union with the Messiah that when they speak it will be as though the Lord Himself has spoken because we are one with Him.

Caught Up

The Enoch community will journey in the land performing time miracles that demonstrate His splendor. We see an example of this in the life of Phillip. Phillip had been sent by the angel of the Lord to minister to a man of Ethiopia in Gaza, a eunuch of great authority under Candace the queen of the Ethiopians.

The Spirit directed Philip to overtake his chariot, where the man was worshiping and reading. Philip proceeded to minister to the man, guiding him in the way of truth, preaching Jesus as they journeyed toward the water where he baptized him. The ministry of Philip was smooth and time-efficient. The angel of the Lord led him, and he followed. His experiences were complete with favor and authority.

After baptizing the man, they came out of the water, and the Spirit of the Lord caught Philip away so that the eunuch no longer saw him but went on his way, rejoicing. Philip was found at Azotus. And passing through, he preached in all the cities till he came to Caesarea.

It was approximately 34 miles (59.8 kilometers) between Gaza and Caesarea, where Philip ended up. This miraculous demonstration of supernatural translation, or teleportation as it is often referred to, is an example of what we can expect to see the Enoch community of the last days frequently do.

This description of being caught away is a Greek word *harpazo* (Strong's #726), which means "caught up" or "snatched away" or "suddenly taken by force."

While influencing within the land, Philip was translated in the Spirit to preach Jesus and identify those whom the Lord will gather, encouraging them in the true knowledge of God. Time miracles will not be demonstrated for selfish gain but for carrying the true knowledge of God to a generation. In these latter days, many saints will be "suddenly taken" in the Spirit to provide adequate ministry in a short amount of time like Philip, fulfilling the prophecy that knowledge will increase.

TIME AND LIGHT

Christ spoke of the darkest hour when there will be false prophets and false christs rising to show great signs and wonders to deceive. There will be great tribulation such as has not been since the beginning of the world until this time, no, nor ever shall be. And unless those days were shortened, no flesh would be saved; but for the elect's sake, those days will be shortened.

There will be a realignment in the Spirit that will affect the earth's natural conditions, bringing sudden inconsistencies; time as we know it will be confused. Planets and stars will transgress their order and not appear at the season authorized. The fruit of the earth will be backward and lose its glory. The sun will be darkened, and the moon will not give its light, the stars of Heaven will fall, and the powers in Heaven will be shaken (see Matt. 24). Though there will be this time of trouble, such as never was, delay will lose its power. The people shall be delivered, everyone who is found written in the book.

They will then see a radiance shining more brightly than the typical order of light. The Son of Man will come in the clouds with great power and glory. He will send His angels and gather together His elect from the four winds, from the farthest part of earth to the farthest part of Heaven.

Beloved, do not let this one thing escape your notice: With the Lord a day is like a thousand years, and a thousand years are like a day. The Lord is not slow in keeping His promise and we will arrive to the culmination of all these things. His Beloved will operate in the realm of the

Spirit to come to the unity of the faith and the fullness of the knowledge of God, which is our timeline.

The remnant will have authority both inside and outside the realm of time. The understanding that we are not bound to time will give them the authority to move through time to accomplish all that must be accomplished before the Lord's return (see Matt. 24; Mark 13:24; 2 Pet. 3; Book of Enoch 2, 80).

ELIJAH

Time miracles will be a form of protection and hiddenness for the elect during times of darkest pain. The Enoch community will be protected, "snatched away," and placed into safe locations under the authority of the Lord. During darkest warfare some will be "caught up" in the Spirit to literally abide in the shadow of the Almighty or be "suddenly taken" from trouble and supernaturally placed into safe geographical locations. For He is not bound by time and can stop it, speed it up, or pull them from it at His design.

We see another example of supernatural transportation in 1 Kings 18 during the days of Elijah. Elijah had prophesied rain, and behold a cloud as small as a man's hand was coming up from the sea. He commanded Ahab to prepare his chariot and go ahead to Jezreel. It was not long before the sky grew black with wind and heavy rains. Ahab rode and went to Jezreel. The Lord's grace was on Elijah as he girded up his loins and miraculously outran Ahab to Jezreel (see 1 Kings 18). It is obvious that the Lord was with Elijah for him to outrun the chariot in the dark of a storm. Perhaps God performed this time miracle to protect Elijah from the storm, or maybe He did it to protect him from his enemies. The Scripture does not say. Perhaps God did it just because He can. One thing is clear: the prophet Elijah journeyed with God, glorifying His name and demonstrating His power. The Lord Most High certainly gave him authority over time and space, enabling Elijah to go the distance in a short amount of time.

Passing through Their Midst

When the Creator of the universe walked the earth in human form, He performed miracles, signs and wonders, releasing Truth and inspiring hope. In the power of the Spirit He came to Nazarath, His sharp word of wisdom brought correction that massively offended the religious spirit.

In time the religious zealots' ire rose. They got up and drove Him out of the city and up on a hill planning to throw Him down the cliff. There was however an appointed time for His crucifixion, a time ordained by the Father to fulfill every prophecy, as the final sacrifice, yielding His Spirit on our behalf. Any advances to do so would not prosper before the fullness of time.

With the ability to stop and silence all the wickedness, Messiah could have shown His authority in powerful outward demonstrations like fire from Heaven or a whirlwind to remove His enemies. Instead, He showed His authority over space and time: "Passing through their midst, He went His way" (Luke 4:30).

Front-runners leading the way in the new day will not only explore realms unseen but will demonstrate great leadership through their pursuit to abide with God. The abiding will result in both transparency and invisibility. Even as Jesus *passed "through their midst,"* so will these leaders cross through battles while remaining unseen by the enemy.

Such occurrences will be manifested outwardly by utilizing the authority granted to defy the typical laws of time. Also, this invisibility will be in the realm of the Spirit, angelic warring and breaking through on their behalf—legions of angels released by God to deter wicked forces.

> *A thousand may fall at your side and ten thousand at your right hand, but it shall not approach you. You will only look on with your eyes and see the recompense of the wicked. ...For He will give His angels charge concerning you, to guard you in all your ways* (Psalm 91:7-8,11).

It has happened all through history, the Lord hiding His Beloved from evil. Time and time again, the Lord's loving hand responds with protection for those who long to abide.

The Weapon of Invisibility

In this recent edition of the Christian periodical *The Connection*, the story is told of God's miraculous protection of Corrie ten Boom when He made her invisible while being transferred into a Nazi concentration camp:

> Corrie ten Boom was a middle-aged spinster who led an uneventful life as a watchmaker in Haarlem, Holland. When's Hitler's armies conquered much of Europe in the early 1940s, Corrie's brother, a minister in the Dutch Reformed Church, began to shelter Jewish refugees. Eventually, as German troops occupied Holland, Corrie decided to help too, by hiding Jewish friends in a secret passage within her home, until they could be smuggled out of the country.
>
> Gradually, the Ten Boom household became the center of the city's resistance movement, with hundreds of Jews passing through, and some being hidden permanently. "My room resembled a beehive, a sort of clearinghouse for supply and demand," she wrote in *A Prisoner, and Yet....*
>
> On Feb. 28, 1944, Corrie, her sister, Betsie, and their father were betrayed and arrested. Although the Gestapo searched their house, the secret room had been so cleverly designed that

they could find no evidence of smuggling. Since the Ten Booms refused to reveal the house's hiding place, they were convicted of stealing food-ration cards and sent to prison. (All but one of their guests ultimately reached safety.)

Corrie's father lived for only 10 days after being sentenced, but for Corrie and Betsie, the next year was hell itself. And yet through their indomitable spirit and firm faith in God, the sisters brought hope and kindness to many suffering prisoners. To Corrie's knowledge, she never saw an angel "in the flesh," but she found evidence of angelic intervention.

At one point, as she and other inmates arrived at the dreaded Ravensbruck, a women's extermination camp, Corrie realized in horror that all their possessions, including warm clothes, were being taken from them. They would freeze in this desolate wasteland. And what of her little Bible? She wore it on a string around her neck, and it had been her consolation through the hard days thus far. But surely it would be confiscated.

Before it was Corrie's turn to be stripped and searched, she asked permission to use the bathroom. There, she wrapped the Bible in Betsie's and her woolen underwear, laid the bundle in a corner, and returned to the row of waiting

> prisoners. Later, after Corrie and Betsie had been dressed in the prison's regulation undershirt and dress, Corrie hid the roll of warm underwear and her Bible under her clothes. It bulged considerably, but she prayed, Lord, send your angels to surround me.
>
> Then, realizing that angels were spirits, she amended the prayer: Lord, do not let them be transparent today, for the guards must not see me!
>
> Calmly, she then passed the guards. Everyone else in line was searched from side to side and top to bottom, every bulge and crease investigated. The woman in front of Corrie had hidden a woolen vest under her dress, and it was immediately spotted and confiscated. Behind her, Betsie was searched.
>
> But Corrie passed without being touched—or even looked at—by anyone. It was as if no one saw her in line. At the outer door, as a second row of guards felt the body of each prisoner, she was again unnoticed.[1]

In this miraculous account of God's faithfulness to Corrie ten Boom, invisibility was her weapon. I believe the Lord was compelled by her desire to abide with Him. She was a pillar in her community of people and a beautiful expression of courage during one of history's darkest horrors. She defied the laws of space and time because her faith in God was greater than the threats of wickedness at every turn.

There is a radical revelation about time and its authority coming to a community that dares to believe. In the days ahead those purposed to abide will have an expansion of authority in the Spirit, giving more space and room to tell His story.

There are many examples of miracles where the Lord's Beloved is protected, hidden, invisible, or transported. In many occasions time appears to stand still.

SUPERNATURAL TRANSPORT

Many years ago I had made plans to go to the next town over for a few days and tuck away with the Lord. He had promised me revelation, rest, and hope during our weekend together. The Lord was clear that I was to stay with Him on a certain weekend. I rearranged all my plans to ensure that weekend was set aside for only me and God.

I had heard of a terrible snowstorm that had targeted the land, projected to cover both towns. I did not have an adequate car for the snow at this point in my life, so I did my best to get out of town ahead of the storm. The downpour of white came earlier than expected and right in the middle of my travel. The land was not just blanketed with a simple dusting, but in a flash these blizzard conditions were blinding. I remembered that some had warned this storm would last three days straight and never cease. While I did not ignore those rumors, I was not prepared for the severity.

What started as a sunny clear day was suddenly sheets of white across my windshield, my wipers freezing every ten seconds. Driving slowly, blindly navigating, and unable to see one foot beyond the car, I stopped every 30 seconds to wipe the windows and clear the ice. I pulled over just three miles from the town I left. I was communicating with friends requesting prayer. Any chance of being rescued was not an option; this was not the weather to venture out in.

Now understanding that the projected blizzard was, in fact, as bad as they said, I was wracking my brain, determining my next plan of action. I now understood that this would go on for days without pause, so parking and waiting it out was not an option. On a normal day, my hotel was a simple 30-minute drive away. In this weather, if there were a way, it would take hours to arrive at my destination. I was beginning to get nervous, though I knew the Lord had promised to abide with me. I was desperate for Him to come and stay awhile, desperate to receive from His heart. Instead of letting fear rise, I decided to remember who He is! I contacted those friends and told them to pray that I would arrive at my destination somehow. Going back was not an option for the storm had covered all the land.

I sat there in that car with only one really good option—believe.

I spoke to the Lord with great courage and surprisingly without skepticism: "If ever You have transported me, transport me now."

I had experienced times of supernatural travel but always as a surprise from the Lord and not because I prayed or purposed for it. This time, it seemed to be my only hope. Just months earlier, I had prophesied this storm and the impactful spiritual breakthrough that was coming for the Bride of Christ. I knew the snow was definite. The storm would be a sign that the Lord would do something new, even making a roadway in the wilderness, rivers in the desert (see Isa. 43:19). He would make something out of nothing and cause His people to praise Him. It was a beckon to abide with Him.

I proceeded to put the car back in drive and creep along in an attempt to make it safely to my destination, still hopeful to be supernaturally transported. But the ground was solid with ice. Suddenly, I looked up and saw the welcome sign to the town, which should have been still 20 miles away. The Lord had done it. Time as we know it did not reflect the distance I had traveled. In His love for me, He not only protected me from the storm, saving me from dangerous travel on icy roads, but He transported me through time so that I might abide with Him. That storm went down in the history books as one of the worst storms to ever hit that region in a hundred years.

A few of you reading this will one day experience such travel if not already. There are times when the Lord helps us arrive somewhere safely, and we endure the rough roads and weary travel. But there is a day coming when experiences like this one will be more frequent. In desperation to not only survive but to abide, His Beloved will be encouraged in the journey to true knowledge. Abiding in the shadow of the Almighty, an infilling of God's presence is available. This will perpetuate the establishment of authority, shelter, divine kingship, and the ability to rule directly from the will of God.

NOTE

1. Joan Wester Anderson, "Corrie ten Boom Receives an Invisible Invitation," *The Connection*, January, 4, 2020, https://gettheconnection.online/2020/01/04/corrie-ten-boom-receives-an-invisiable-invitation.

CHAPTER 8

THE POWER OF THE NAME

FIRST LOVE

First love's song is a melody, beckoning the Beloved into perfect union—the union found in abiding rest and knitted in vulnerability. He will betroth the Beloved to Himself forever in righteousness and justice, in loving-kindness and compassion. The chosen of the Lord will present herself as one alive from the dead, unified and without blemish. Holy and spiritual affection will bond the remnant of His people to one another, pulling on the violent wind of His Spirit. On Pentecost the violent rushing wind rendered the entire house awe-inspired, setting up the Bride in confidence for her created destiny. Behold He is doing something new. Now! It will spring forth, winds of His Spirit will again reveal and mobilize a chosen generation to execute in confidence the destiny created for them for such a time as this. A magnitude of wisdom from the spirit of wisdom that has never been released will motivate a congregation and lead them in the ways of the Father.

Pure affection between brethren will result in an increase of the reverential fear of the Lord. For it reaches to the depths of first love's song and pulls the strings of David's harp. It is loving-kindness in generous proportion that will ultimately release His fire in generous proportion and establish a community on solid ground.

Acts 2 depicts the perfect breakthrough of one large spiritual family devoted to prayer and unity. Men and women gathered in the upper room, waiting in desperation for a design known well only by their spirit—a blueprint that would stretch far beyond human comprehension. In a moment, the union found in their abiding rest pulled on holy fire and brought forth the order of their function individually. We are told that there appeared to them divided (distributed) tongues, as of fire, and one sat (appointed) upon each of them individually (see Acts 2:3). The language here indicates a divine appointment. Fire came and appointed each of them individually. To each a function, a distribution of authority, a distinct and clear order. *"For the equipping of the saints for the work of service, to the building up of the body of Christ; until we all attain to the unity of the faith, and of the knowledge of the Son of God"* (Eph. 4:12-13).

On the day of Pentecost, in accordance with the order of Heaven, Peter called for repentance and for each to be immersed in the *name* of Yeshua, thus receiving the Holy Spirit.

> *Peter said to them, "Repent, and each of you be baptized* [immersed] *in the name of Jesus Christ"* (Acts 2:38).

The revelation of the full identity of this name will transform a generation and bring in this massive harvest and the continued building up of the Body in love. No longer susceptible to deceitful scheming or the trickery of men, understanding the power in His name, we will attain to the measure of the stature which belongs to the fullness of Christ. For those with ears to hear, the revelation of the true knowledge of the Son of God will encourage His Beloved to receive her true identity, made in His image and a carrier of the Name above all names.

Peter highlights the power that is in the Name. The Name of One who makes known to us the ways of life and carries the full power of resurrection. Eternal Lord, the Lord of spirits, the Spirit of the Lord, perfect love, the fullness of His nature, character, and sevenfold spirit. The spirit of wisdom and understanding, the spirit of counsel and strength, the spirit of knowledge, and the fear of the Lord, who slays the wicked with the breath of His lips. There is complete power in His name. The spirit of might motivates the hearts of men radically to display

His splendor and bring forth good fruit—expressions of life from the womb of understanding for a holy people that we would increase in awe forever more.

Reverent submission to the Name of Yeshua will encourage the ways of first love and keep the fire of revival burning in the hearts of men. Amidst individual expression of His love, the Beloved must continue in the ways of abiding rest. For the Name holds both rest and power.

The book of Revelation indicates an urgency from the Lord to repent and return to this first love:

> *You have perseverance and have endured for My name's sake, and have not grown weary. But I have this against you, that you have left your first love. Therefore remember from where you have fallen, and repent and do the deeds you did at first; or else I am coming to you and will remove your lampstand out of its place—unless you repent* (Revelation 2:3-5).

Peter encouraged the congregation to repent and be overtaken by the power in the Name, a true demonstration and revelation of first love. In the book of Revelation, the Lord urges His Beloved to again repent, do what they did at first—be overtaken and immersed by the power of His name. The sevenfold spirit of God is in the Name. Irreverent dismissal of this power will result in the removal of the lampstand—the removal of access to the seven spirits of God.

> *Therefore remember from where you have fallen, and repent and do the deeds you did at first* (Revelation 2:5).

This is not only a plea but a warning from the heart of the Father, beckoning the Beloved to return to reverent submission. The reverential fear of the Lord is not only an attribute of the Name but a requirement to fully operate in its power. To be immersed in the Name is to mindfully revere Him and express first love as we did at once.

Peter referenced King David: *"You have made known to me the ways of life; You will make me full of gladness with Your presence"* (Acts 2:28).

It is without a doubt the true regret of the soul to deny the power in the Name, for in the Name is the fullness of life, gladness, and loving-kindness: Yeshua—a true inspiration, sparing the Beloved of dreadful separation from the Father. First love's song is an invitation for the union found in abiding rest. It will bring forth restoration and continued access to His sevenfold spirit, which is the lampstand (see Rev. 2:5). To him who overcomes they will be granted to eat of the tree of life.

A revelation of the power in the Name is being released in this new day—a revelation of the sevenfold spirit of God.

> *"And it shall be in the last days," God says, "that I will pour forth of My Spirit on all mankind"* (Acts 2:17).

His invisible attributes, eternal power, and divine nature have been clearly seen, so we are without excuse. For there are many who have known God, though they did not honor Him as God or give thanks, but they became futile in their speculations and their foolish heart was darkened (see Rom. 1:20-21).

There is an urgent call to return to first love. The overcomers will position themselves in reverence to receive full comprehension of the power and nature of the Name. In this appointed time, a remnant will receive mysteries hidden in the Name and execute the authority of Yeshua. Paul Keith describes the magnitude of this reward:

> It would be difficult to overstate the importance and the power of His name. In Revelation 3:12 the Lord rewards those who overcome to be inscribed with the name of My God, and the name of the city of My God, the new Jerusalem, which comes down out of Heaven from My God, and My new name.

Smith Wigglesworth: Raising Lazarus

This truth was evident in the life of Smith Wigglesworth and John G. Lake, who were clearly carriers of the

Name, likely having received of these hidden mysteries. Smith Wigglesworth had a true reverence for the Name of Jesus and a humble confidence in its power, which led to a ministry of life-changing miracles and healings.

In his book *Ever-Increasing Faith* he shares of an experience in Wales when the Lord graced him with the honor of touching the power of the Name. The power of the Name was demonstrated to and through Wigglesworth and a group of faithful servants when a man called Lazarus was raised up to healing and strength.

A leader who had spent his days working in a tin mine and his nights preaching had collapsed and gone into consumption. For four years he was helpless and seemingly hopeless, being taken care of for every need. He was bedridden and unable to dress or even feed himself. The people of his community had lost hope; however, there were two young men who had a little faith. They had seen the works of God performed through Smith Wigglesworth and his team and reached out on behalf of Lazarus.

Wigglesworth inquired of the Lord for some time and was then directed by God to go to the Welsh village and raise up Lazarus.

Upon arrival he was not well received, for the people did not believe. A man of no faith directed Wigglesworth back to the man called Lazarus. It was with obvious disdain that the man said, "The moment you see him you will be ready to go home. Nothing will hold you."

Wigglesworth recorded that in the natural that viewpoint was true, for Lazarus was lifeless. The spirit of death consumed him.

There were difficult conditions in the Welsh village. Unbelief was rampant, and the power of the devil had even come upon Wigglesworth with similar symptoms as Lazarus. He cried out to God to deliver him; meanwhile, he proceeded to find people who were brave enough to pray. It took some doing, but he was able to gather seven who believed.

He contended in prayer and fasting for hours on behalf of Lazarus until he felt the release of the Lord. In great favor and courage, eight total servants went to the sick man's room and circled his bed. Wigglesworth directed them, "We are not going to pray, we are just going to use the name of Jesus." Kneeling down, he whispered one word: "Jesus! Jesus! Jesus!"

It was a process to break unbelief off of Lazarus; still, the Lord had spoken to Wigglesworth and gave him a special endurance to see this through. They repeated the process, speaking the Name while believing in the power and fullness of it. They did this process over and over again, speaking the Name—"Jesus! Jesus! Jesus!"—and believing the power. The sixth time the power fell on the man, and his lips began to move. Tears filled the crevices of his eyes, soon pouring down his face. In this moment Wigglesworth spoke to him. "The power of God is here; it is yours to accept it." The man was filled with remorse: "I have been bitter in my heart, and I know I have grieved the Spirit of God. Here I am helpless. I cannot lift my hands, nor even lift a spoon to my mouth." Wigglesworth called for the man to repent, and the virtue of the Lord went right through him.

I believe that all that was in the Name went through the man in that moment. The nature, power, essence, and virtue of God were revealed and demonstrated. Eight faithful ones came together in unity and believed the power in the Name, thus releasing that power to raise Lazarus after four years of trial and torment. It was repentance that ultimately delivered him, restoring him to his connection to the Father and access to all that is in the Name.

Wigglesworth was undaunted by their unbelief and, despite trials of his own, pursued healing at the direction and promise of the Lord—the promise also found in the Name.

In time the events of this miracle spread throughout the village and district, drawing people to see Wigglesworth for themselves and hear his testimony. The Lord was mindful to bring salvation to many.

John G. Lake: Waves of Holy Glory

John G. Lake was responsible for raising over 1,000,000 converts, 625 churches, and 1,250 preachers in 5 years of ministry! The healings that took place during his ministry had an obvious impact on his town of Spokane,

Washington, so much that it was considered the healthiest town in America during this time. Even with the ministry of healing powerfully working through him, he had an ever-increasing desire to enter in and receive of the fullness, the true knowledge of God.

Early on in his ministry he had an encounter that symbolizes the nature and power of the Name. He describes this transformative encounter and the state of his heart with honesty and vulnerability in the book *Apostle to Africa.*

> Eight years passed after God revealed Jesus the healer to me. I had been practicing the ministry of healing. During that eight years every answer to prayer, every miraculous touch of God, every response of my own soul to the Spirit had created within me a more intense longing for an intimacy and a consciousness of God, like I felt the disciples of Jesus and the primitive church had possessed.
>
> Shortly after my entrance into the ministry of healing, while attending a service where the necessity for the Baptism of the Holy Spirit was presented, as I knelt in prayer and reconsecration to God, an anointing of the Spirit came upon me. Waves of Holy Glory passed through my being, and I was lifted into a new realm of God's presence and power. After this, answers

> to prayer were frequent and miracles of healing occurred from time to time. I felt myself on the borderland of a great spiritual realm, but was unable to enter in fully, so my nature was not satisfied with the attainment.[1]

Many leaders of our day are in this same "borderland," carrying within them a holy hunger to go beyond the fringes and access the Spirit without measure—not only able to move in the gifts but to be imbued in the full comprehension of His name, for all things have been given into His hands.

> *He who comes from above is above all, he who is of the earth is from the earth and speaks of the earth. He who comes from heaven is above all. What He has seen and heard, of that He testifies; and no one receives His testimony. He who has received His testimony has set his seal to this, that God is true. For He whom God has sent speaks the words of God; for He gives the Spirit without measure. The Father loves the Son and has given all things into His hand* (John 3:31-35).

John G. Lake set aside hours, dedicating specific times of prayer, contending for the baptism of the Holy Spirit—complete immersion of His name. He learned the discipline of perseverance as he submitted himself for months in focused prayer and meditation. It became easy for him to detach and yield up his spirit. Eventually, he partnered with his brothers in the faith, and in union they agreed to contend together for the baptism.

This is how he described it in the book *Apostle to Africa*:

> I had not been praying five minutes until the light of God began to shine around me, I found myself in a center of an arc of light ten feet in diameter, the whitest light in all the universe. So white! Oh how it spoke of purity. The remembrance of that whiteness, that wonderful whiteness, has been the ideal that has stood before my soul, of the purity of the nature of God ever since.
>
> Then a Voice began to talk to me out of that light. There was no form. And the Voice began to remind me of this incident and that incident of disobedience to my parents, from a child; of my obstinacy, and dozens of instances when God brought me up to the line of absolutely putting my body, soul, and spirit upon the altar forever. I had my body upon the altar for ten years, and I had been a minister of the Gospel. But when the Lord comes, He opens to the soul the depths that have never been touched in your life. Do you know that after I was baptized in the Holy Ghost, things opened up in the

> depths of my nature that remained untouched in all my life, and that which was shadowy, distant, and hazy became real. God got up close and let His light shine into me.[2]

It is an amazing destiny to be known by God. For there is no creature hidden from His sight, but all things are open and laid bare to the One who discerns the thoughts and intentions of our heart (see Heb. 4:12). When the Righteous One reveals Himself before the eyes of the chosen ones, there is an impartation as powerful as flaming lights, causing their mouths to overflow with blessing and their lips to magnify the Name above all names—the Name in which is the Lord of spirits, fulfilling the complete nature of God.

John G. Lake was imbued with the very Spirit of the Christ, which launched him into deeper intimacy and complete transparency, including miracles and healings of massive proportion. He concludes his revelation with light beautifully and describes how God compelled him, drawing him into a walk of intimacy and compassion:

> Shortly after my baptism in the Holy Spirit, a working of the Spirit commenced in me, that seemed to have for its purpose the revelation of the nature of Jesus Christ to and in me. Through this tuition and remolding of the Spirit a great tenderness for mankind was awaken in my soul. The desire to proclaim the message of Christ,

> and demonstrate His power to save and bless, grew in my soul until my life was swayed by this overwhelming passion.[3]

In the atmosphere of the reverential fear of the Lord, righteousness will never falter and honor will never fail. In His presence is fullness of joy; at His right hand, pleasures forevermore (see Ps. 16:11). Our spirit longs for complete saturation of His presence, for in His name there are no limits. Rewards, gifts, transformative light, ultimate peace, and access to His knowledge, which extends infinitely. There is a mysterious infusion coming to a people; few have already encountered fragments of its glory. A reality unwritten and inexpressible in words, for it is deity unmatchable. A reality Daniel and Enoch have seen, Moses understood, and Elijah witnessed. Words cannot adequately capture the moments of encounter or the vastness of His Kingdom. There are stories of the heroes who have gone before us who understood what it takes to be yielded vessels. They went in deep, beyond the outskirts of this power. These stories motivate us to pursue the unseen realm and express the glory beyond the veil. Submerged in His name, the courageous will submit what is not relevant, surrender their will, and yield up their spirit. Eventually they will enter into the full and true knowledge of the Son of God.

> The greatest human attainment in all the world is for a life to be so surrendered to Him that the name of God Almighty will be glorified through that life.
>
> —Kathryn Kuhlman

Notes

1. Gordon Lindsay, compiler, *John G. Lake: Apostle to Africa* (Dallas, TX: Christ for the Nations, Inc., 1995), 16.
2. Ibid.
3. Ibid., 20.

Chapter 9

Tongues of Fire: An Agreement with Destiny

Zimbabwe, Africa, is one of my favorite places on the earth. Children's laughter, village unity, perfect sunsets, and humble servants. True majesty is woven in the crevices of the landscape, and great love embodies lovers. Sadly, poverty has raged against the villages, leaving the land dry and produce scarce. Though the spiritual battle over those grounds is burdensome and the sorrow is apparent, a generation is being formed by the hands of God. Royalty will rise from the depths and change the very face of the nation. I believe in the shepherding nature of the Father to gather the Beloved from every tribe, nation, and kingdom and set them in the ways of life.

I first saw Zimbabwe's royalty in a dream long before I ever touched the land—a girl representing the future vision of Zimbabwe, an African queen in regal attire, barefoot in the middle of a remote village. I remember the beauty of the dress; the design is forever embedded in my memory. Swirls of burgundy and gold draped around her ankles as she stood tall in a field of people. I understood she was royalty of the grandest family and graced for political reign. The dream highlighted her feet as I washed them with muddy African soil. Humbled by her superiority, I began to prophesy her destiny. The message of hope for a nation poured forth from my lips as I encouraged her to walk as one of noble birth.

I held this dream quiet in my heart and reverently before the Lord in prayer. I did not speak about the dream but merely pondered the reality of praying for African royalty. Not long after, an intercessor recited my entire dream back to me. Remember, I had never spoken of it with anyone. She shared details that nobody had known, only the Lord. I took this seriously and paid close attention to the details of my dream and her word for me. I had a strong sense the Lord was going to connect me with an African woman who represented the future vision of Zimbabwe. I went on a mission to find her.

Three months later I was there in Zimbabwe, preparing to speak at a tent meeting. Three hundred to four hundred villagers attended the meeting, rocking worship African style—dancing, singing, stomping, and praising with all that was within them, with broken down drum sets and sound systems that pale compared to American lavishness. The setting of the village perfectly depicted certain details in my dream. I was excitedly awaiting the culmination of it all. There in Zimbabwe, agreeing with God's destiny for this place, I felt inspiration growing within me.

Surrounded by many villagers whose praise undoubtedly shook the heavens, I had set the dream aside and was appreciating the energy and joy of the villagers. Nineteen years of age, a young girl approached me and began asking questions. She was showing gratitude and requesting a picture. We shared a moment behind flashing camera lights. This beautiful and vibrant young lady began to speak to me from the depths of the Spirit with the humility of David. I heard in her the authority of Esther and the loyalty of Ruth. Suddenly, as though something had hit me on the head with a stick, I felt it drop into me:

"This is her."

I listened longer as she spoke; her English was stronger than many of the other villagers, yet Shona was woven into her speech. I saw the sincerity in her eyes and her genuine love for the Father. Eventually, I asked her name. She shared with boldness, "I. Am. Vision." I was truly undone. The Lord quite literally sent to me the "Vision" of Zimbabwe.

Several days later, she had agreed for me to pray over her. After one of the services, she and her mother and a handful of intercessors joined me in the village's open field. The villagers kindly brought a chair out into the open, propped up sideways on the land's rocky part. The African queen took her seat. The intercessors began to pray, and her mother knelt at her side, holding a scarf that matched perfectly to the regal dress worn in my dream. The Lord matched every detail.

Vision's smile joined the portrait of stars in the endless African sky, lighting up the field where we prayed. I bowed before her and began to wash her feet with the dirt of the land. While sharing the message the Lord had prepared for her, suddenly I saw in the spirit a bright light straight from the heavens resting upon her head. This pillar of light appeared as a portal or a window of access. I could feel angels ascending and descending on her behalf. She began to speak in another language that did not sound like Shona—a language of freedom, a spiritual tongue unique and distinct.

I discerned situations in her life and spoke of them in the prophecy. Her mother confirmed that the description of her trials that were given to me by the Holy Spirit were accurate. She fell at her feet, weeping and praying for her daughter. She, too, broke into a language of freedom.

I knew in this moment that they were joining Heaven's song over Vision. I found out later that this was the first time Vision had received the baptism of the Holy Spirit. Perhaps she was coming into agreement with her prophetic promise. I have since pondered her unique situation and the power behind her spiritual language. I believe the spiritual sound she released was a song of praise and a moment of agreement.

Amos 3:3 says, *"Can two walk together, unless they are agreed?"* (NKJV). That word *agreed* is a Hebrew word, *yaad,* which means "appointment." As I compared this to the day of Pentecost recorded in the book of Acts, a deeper understanding of the importance of the baptism of fire was unveiled.

> *And suddenly there came from Heaven a noise like a violent rushing wind, and it filled the whole house where they were sitting. And there appeared to them tongues as of fire distributing themselves, and they rested on each one of them. And they were all filled with the Holy Spirit and began to speak with other tongues, as the Spirit was giving the utterance* (Acts 2:2-4).

The distribution of the spiritual language rested on each of them. That word *each* means "separately, distinctly as opposed to severally, or as a group."

On that day in Pentecost, they were inspired to move into their divine purpose. They received this calling as they were filled with the Holy Spirit and began to prophesy. Each member was given the language of Heaven. At this moment, they came into agreement with their appointed time and released a song of praise unto the Lord.

In the same way, Vision praised the Lord humbly and agreed with what was spoken for her life. Her mother also joined the Lord's message and released Vision into the calling.

From Declaration to Operation

Hannah contended with God for a child despite a barren womb. She promised to submit him to the Lord all of his days if God would grant her this gift. After beckoning the Lord, He heard her cry, and in due time she gave birth to a son and named him Samuel, saying, *"Because I have asked him of the Lord"* (1 Sam. 1:20).

She released Samuel into the ministry at a very young age. He went on to be priest, judge, and prophet, and the Lord let none of his words fall to the ground. Everything he prophesied came to pass. Samuel is a type of true apostolic leadership. Paul Keith shares an encounter where the Lord reveals the coming apostolic:

> Recently, the Lord gave a very compelling prophetic experience or vision to depict the season in which we are living. In it, a prophet we know and have utmost respect for entered a room of leaders being prepared for this next season of the Spirit. This mature and loyal prophet stood before the leaders and announced with great power and strength, "The Apostolic is coming." As he did, a voice of ultimate authority echoed

> from Heaven, "The Apostolic is coming." With that affirmation, the prophet continued, "We had better get a good understanding of apostolic ministry under us, for it will be on top of us before we know it. Samuel is a type of this apostolic leadership. The Lord did let none of his words fall to the ground nor did he beg his bread from the people."

Samuel's destiny was ordained by God and called in by Hannah. Her cries in intercession not only confirmed her assignment and Samuel's, but continue to impact generations. Samuel is a picture of the restored apostolic government that will represent the last-day ministry.

After Samuel's birth, Hannah released a true prophetic song with a reverential sound. It was a song of agreement and a sound of rejoicing.

In intercession, prior to his birth, she called forth his appointment.

In celebration after his birth, she agreed with that divine appointment. She moved from revelation to operation.

This was her assignment.

Samuel is symbolic of a community that will move in true apostolic authority. In this hour a group of true apostolic leaders will move into operation. It is their appointed time.

Acts 2:3 says, *"Then there appeared to them divided tongues, as of fire, and one sat upon each of them"* (NKJV).

This word *sat* is the Greek word *kathizó,* which means, "I make to sit; I set, I appoint." It was the moment of appointment.

Paul Keith's grasp of the feasts beautifully seals this revelation:

> To fully understand the events that occurred on the Day of Pentecost we must also examine the directions given to Moses concerning the "Feasts of the Lord." The Hebrew word for *feasts* is *moed* meaning "divine appointments." The Scriptures also tell us these dates as celebrated from the days of Moses up until the time of Christ were holy convocations. The Hebrew word for *holy convocation* is *miqra.* This word does not only mean a gathering of people but a dress rehearsal. For many years Israel celebrated the Feast of Pentecost as a dress rehearsal for the divine appointment that would occur following the resurrection of Christ when 120 were filled with the Holy Spirit and came into a union experience with the Living God.

Directly following the baptism of fire, many of the people marveled in amazement while others began to mock, accusing them of being drunk. Peter stood in defense of the Holy Spirit and delivered a powerful message to the congregation—recalling what was prophesied by the prophet Joel:

> *For these are not drunk, as you suppose, since it is only the third hour of the day. But this is what was spoken by the prophet Joel: "And it shall come to pass in the last days, says God, that I will pour out My Spirit on all flesh; your sons and your daughters shall prophesy...And on My menservants and on My maidservants I will pour out My Spirit in those days; and they shall prophesy"* (Acts 2:15-18 NKJV).

Peter was clarifying that what they had just witnessed was a fulfillment of what was prophesied by the prophet Joel, further supporting the narrative that the tongues of fire were a process of prophetic agreement in addition to thankfulness to God.

A moment of divine appointment is upon us. In intercession, we called in the winds of change and pursued our allotted time. Now we agree with that which has been appointed to us. We will move from declaration to operation, and the result will be glorious. In songs of thanksgiving, we will praise Him and agree with our appointment already ordained by God.

IRREVOCABLE

In January 2018 I was driving down a mountain, carefully minding the curves of the mountain roads. The snow began to fall incessantly; the roads were quickly freezing. It was an unexpected change of weather. I had both children in the back seat, and they were young. I was praying quietly for the Lord's help, as the car I was driving was not equipped for this kind of weather. It was all happening very fast; simple snowflakes quickly became treacherous blizzard conditions.

I continued in prayer, believing the Lord would see us through. My car hit a patch of ice and started fishtailing back and forth. No longer in any control, I called out to God. A different car was approaching just 50 yards in front with a head-on approach and nowhere to retreat. Instantly, my cries hit a deeper level of desperation. As I called out to Him, I suddenly saw in the spirit the destiny of each of my children. Their lives played out from beginning to end. I heard a voice shake me to the core:

"But I already said."

When He said "*I*," it was like a thunder that roared throughout the atmosphere, shaking the heavens and the earth.

> *The adversaries of the Lord shall be broken in pieces; from Heaven He will thunder against them* (1 Samuel 2:10 NKJV).

At that moment, my children began to break out into a spiritual language. It was a song of freedom. The car miraculously straightened out, and we seemed to be in the clear only for a brief moment.

Before long, we drove across another patch of ice, which sent us plummeting toward an oncoming cliff. Again, I cried out with even more vigor than before. I saw their allotted time displayed from beginning to end as though I was watching a recording of their lives. In the back seat, the children were aggressively prophesying in a spiritual tongue. Again, I heard the Lord's roar:

"But I already said!"

This was a promise that He will do everything He said He would do in and through their lives. Again, I was reminded that releasing the ones I love to the Lord is one way I can agree with their destiny.

The Holy Spirit came and sat upon each child. He rested on them and spoke through them songs of praise, deliverance, and destiny. I now understand that they were not only crying out to the Lord for help but agreeing with their calling. God's gifts and His call are irrevocable (see Rom. 11:29).

We do not just agree with the Lord for our own promises; we agree on behalf of people—even promises spoken over lands and regions. For some, this is their complete assignment.

It is with great expectation we await the consummation of all things. We are not interceding for a destiny faintly drawn but rather in accordance with that which is predestined. For He will make His people to inherit the throne of glory (see 1 Sam. 2:8).

CHAPTER 10

ONLY BELIEVE

"Only believe. All things are possible if you'll only believe!"

September 16, 2020, my family and I were in a hotel in Montgomery, Alabama, safely sheltered from Hurricane Sally. There was a powerful surge of fire and storm happening in the United States. The Lord had revealed to us that a hurricane was coming and would destroy the docks of Orange Beach, Alabama. One month prior to the hurricane, we took our final pictures on that dock and appreciated the beautiful memories there.

Hurricane Sally caused a historic wall to rage across the boundaries of the land, leaving $6.25 billion in damage (according to the National Hurricane Center). The Lord had revealed to me many months earlier that He would come like the breakthrough of waters.

Interestingly, the word *sally* means "an action, rushing or bursting forth, a breakthrough." This storm would usher in the prophetic destiny of the land. This noise would somehow bring forth the fulfillment of things believed for and prophesied over that region, specifically Baldwin County. The sense was that the Lord will restore and the people will be rebuilt. *"Again I will build you and you will be rebuilt"* (Jer. 31:4).

We had currently been staying in Oregon, where the West Coast fires had been scorching the land, devastating homes, businesses, and livelihoods. The record-breaking fires of 2020 caused the air quality to rise to hazardous levels, the most severe in the world at that time. We had planned a trip to the Gulf Coast to escape the smoke of Oregon. Though we had a strong sense a storm was coming, the news reports did not indicate that this hurricane would move in the manner that it did, which affected the timing of Sally's arrival. We ended up in Montgomery, fleeing the smoke of the West Coast and waiting out the storm of the Gulf Coast.

We woke early in the morning as Hurricane Sally made landfall. Ironically, Hurricane Sally hit within 1 hour to the day 16 years after Hurricane Ivan, which hit September 16, 2004. A seemingly symbolic demonstration of the end of a story, this completion of a season would launch a people, called by His name, into the greatest displays of glory that land has ever known.

I was awakened early the morning of Sally's arrival, with a compulsion to join the prophetic promises that had been released over Baldwin County. I was coming into agreement with her appointed time. While I was connecting with those prayers of destiny, the eye of the storm hovered over our condo in Orange Beach, Alabama. The storm had a maximum sustained wind of 105 miles per hour.

After coming into agreement with the promise for the land, I was quickly pulled by the Lord into a deep rest, as though a weighted blanket covered me and quieted my prayers. Whether awake or asleep, I do not know, but my spirit was well alive. I heard a sound, heavenly but not angelic, begin to sing the words: "Only believe. All things are possible if you'll only believe!"

I pondered the song's sound and the singer throughout the day. The words were powerful and spoke to the cry of my heart for the Beloved. These words of encouragement ignited something in me beyond intercession power. It seemed to speak to the surge of resurrection power I saw blasting the land.

Let me explain.

"Only believe." These two words continue to impact. The land was troubled and wounded. People across the earth are discouraged—overcome by diseases, wickedness, and pain. We need miracles. This heavenly song brought great encouragement that the Lord will pour out His glory; we need to "only believe."

I understood that this is the song William Branham would often sing. I began asking the Lord to confirm who this messenger was who brought me the song. I had a strong inclination that the voice was Branham's; however, I needed something more to confirm. I know the message was the Father's, and I receive every message from Him with reverence. It was also important for me to know who the messenger was.

I had been asking the Lord for an understanding of Branham's role and influence on the remnant of this hour. I know that what is about to be released on the earth is an expression of prophetic promises of power and authority. It will be glory like Branham ministered. We are now moving into the operation of what has been spoken.

The timing of this message is strategic. The voice and the song motivated belief within me. We will see a move of God!

It has been a battle for the Lord's people to move from intercession power to resurrection power, but the time has come. It is imperative to transition from the mere revelation of the glory into the operation of the glory. What was prophesied is now coming to pass.

A few hours after the visitation, I was given my confirmation. Remember, I asked the Lord to confirm if the messenger was William Branham. We all went out to breakfast, and upon return we noticed a prayer cloth sitting on our hotel desk. It was a William Branham prayer cloth that he had prayed over in 1965 before he passed away. They were prayer cloths given to Paul Keith by a friend of William Branham's named Pearry Green. I stored these cloths in a special drawer in Oregon. There was no chance anyone had packed them for the trip; they were kept in a location only known by me. I certainly had not packed it. The timing of this prayer cloth miraculously appearing on our hotel desk is astounding. How did this cloth show up in an Alabama hotel? It is, without a doubt, supernatural.

The virus, the fires, political turmoil, and the worst hurricane season on record definitely marked 2020 as a year of trial, but it will also be marked in history as the year that changed everything. Tyranny began to be exposed as it rose in the land throughout 2021. Conflict, divisiveness, and fear gripped many; however, the Lord began identifying the remnant and drawing her together in family fashion.

Some churches were silenced in cowardice, while leaders anointed by God were inspired with a spirit of courage. According to Heaven's archives, this is the hour the remnant of God's people began to strengthen their voices with songs of faith. It was the time of the end and the time of the beginning.

A divine orchestration has been called forth by intercessors, the cloud of witnesses, and the Lord Jesus Himself, who makes constant intercession on our behalf. It is the song of resurrection power, and it is setting His

Beloved up for victory. He will touch the nations with shouts of grace.

The Lord, thwarting the plans of the enemy and infringing upon the plans of man, will bring forth the plans of His heart from generation to generation and from the West Coast to the East. He will touch the nations with shouts of grace, and His Word will be fulfilled.

We will join Heaven's song of prophecy: "Only believe. All things are possible if you'll only believe." This is the day of our appointment.

> *Arise, shine; for your light has come, and the glory of the Lord has risen upon you. For behold, darkness will cover the earth and deep darkness the peoples; but the Lord will rise upon you and His glory will appear upon you* (Isaiah 60:1-2).

About Amy Thomas Davis

Amy Thomas Davis was born in Oregon. Her earliest memories of supernatural encounters with the Lord provided revelatory insight for her life and that of her family. At the age of 19 Amy had an encounter with the Father as manifested Love. That event changed her life and inspired her to know and express Him as love. For many years she devoted her life to prophetic intercession. Her experiences in the unseen realm of God have given her insight into who He is and the time and season in which we live. Amy's desire is to see the fullness of God's glory resident upon the radical remnant that will do great exploits. She and her husband, Paul Keith Davis, oversee WhiteDove Ministries, a ministry devoted to preparing and equipping God's people to walk in realms of glory and the fullness of divine destiny.

www.ingramcontent.com/pod-product-compliance
Lightning Source LLC
LaVergne TN
LVHW010932100826
845153LV00001B/14